TREKKING THE BIG PICTURE

ANDREW LOHREY

Copyright © 2013 Andrew Lohrey

www.spiritualstories.net

All rights reserved. No part of this publication may be reproduced, transmitted, or stored in a retrieval system or by any means without the permission in writing from the publisher.

Rishi
Falmouth, Tasmania, 7215
Australia

978-0-9875938-4-9

Cover design and book layout by Michelle Lovi
Cover photographs by Richard Bugg

Keywords: meaning, spirituality, life, mind, consciousness, empathy, meaning of meaning, language, culture

Contents

Preparing for the Trek   vii

1	Mapping the Route	1
2	The Heavenly Peaks	19
3	Climbing Blake's Pass	37
4	Communal Base Camp	55
5	The Weather of Becoming	69
6	Watchout for Whiteouts	81
7	The Valley of Desires	103
8	Ridges of Intellect	115
9	The Alps of Empathy	131
10	The Geology of Love	141
11	The Big Picture	161
12	Postscript	169

Acknowledgments   177

Index   187

Notes on the Author   194

To Amma: a storm of harmony – unutterably sweet,♥

and Amanda: who was the loving, critical confidante for this big picture trek.

♥ Shelly's *Hellas, 179*.

Preparing for the trek

When trekking it is always a good idea to have the right gear, to wear the right clothes and be prepared for sudden changes in the weather. So how should you prepare for this trek?

Firstly, this is a trek across the country of who we are; the territory of being human. The common view has taken over this territory by staking out privacy claims and putting up boundary (de)fences. Yet the claim for the private person is a narrow one and it is often preoccupied with the negative. In contrast, this trek is through the big and positive country of meaning, of how we make meaning and the underlying nature of meaning itself.

The first real difficulty of this trek is finding the will to see the big picture. One way to deal with this is to buy a small daypack and stuff all your old reactive habits in it and then go to a train station and put the daypack in one of the lockers so they are well and truly left behind.

The second recurring difficulty of this trek is to give up seeing yourself as a separate person with a private mind. This limiting view is essentially materialistic. It says you are a statistic in an economic/commercial plan or a physical body in a biological plan. Either way you are small, limited and only important if you have social influence or wealth. This materialistic view is accompanied by tension in the stomach, hunching the shoulders, knitting of the forehead; in a word, stress. Defending this limiting view make us certain we are right while all the time making us miserable, negative, narrow and competitive. This narrow separating view of self is commonly buried within the musty cupboard of the mind so in order to access the big picture it is necessary to take out those hidden predispositions and tendencies, give them a good wash and hang them out to dry.

It goes without saying that some pilgrims on this trek will find the terrain difficult and in some parts almost inaccessible. One way to tackle those broader contextual vistas is to plan ahead so there are plenty of rest periods. Do not try and take in the whole of meaning or Meaning in one burst. Such an effort may cause hypoventilation and possibly disorientation.

In case of bad weather it is important to carry an orientation device. On this trek, the best of these is an open mind but these days they are really hard to find. If you are unable to obtain an open mind then try the delayed response. This is not as good but at least it's much better than getting completely lost using the common but fatal tools of doubt and scepticism.

However, what you should take along for all occasions, no matter the weather, is a good dose of discernment and of course one of those small safety packs, labeled: to thine own self be true. These packs contain effective truth pills that will help inoculate you against frozen will, false prophets, fundamentalism as well as that awful whiteout called objectivity.

Dear reader, this trek is through the politics of eternity and not through the politics of physics or the computations of time and space. The strategy of this trek is sometimes unpleasant to contemporary sensibilities as it includes a critique of materialism, both the scientific as well as the common and garden consumer variety. The approach here is to expose the underlying software language of the ordinary human mind as well as the divine mind of cosmic consciousness. This is the big picture disclosure that involves the states, codes, structures and laws of Meaning. In addition, this trek asks three questions: i) who am I; ii) what is the nature of the Divine; and iii) why are there weeds in the garden of paradise?

The only other advice I can offer you on this pilgrimage is related to the track, which may be rough in places so watch where you are treading, but at the same time keep a weather eye on the higher peaks otherwise you will surely miss the big picture of who you are.

Chapter 1 – Mapping the route

I am sitting in the Waterside Pavilion in Mawson Place in the city of Hobart, meditating. This is the 12 o'clock *No Worries* daily meditation program run by the Gyuto Monks of Tibet.[1] I have been travelling and missed the first five days of the Gyuto visit and now I have come halfway through their program. Gen Lama talks for ten minutes about *Trading Grief* and then we meditate.

I have little grief to trade and find it hard to hear the English translation by Sonam, the younger Tibetan who translates for Gen Lama. I sit at the back of the room in my fog of bad hearing. I have come for the meditation, not the talk. I meditate daily and have come to experience the silence of Gen Lama who, along with the Dalai Lama, walked out of Tibet in 1959. He must be a similar age to the Dalai Lama and looks as if he could be related to him. He sits beneath a picture of the Dalai Lama so I have a double image of almost the same face; same large glasses, same shaved head, the same round face and skin color. As you would expect, the energy in this peaceful room comes from Gen Lama, not the picture.

I came early and for ten minutes before the meditation watched the younger monks play with the children who were there for the period of *Culture for Kids*. I rested my hands on the rail looking down at the young monks seated cross-legged on the floor below me and making various forms with plasticine, and all the while being there, with and for the children. The Mawson Pavilion is a beautiful building that faces east and sits on the edge of a dock full of sailing ships. The sun shines through the windows and the scene is relaxed, full of an easy joyful presence. I merge into the presence so much so that I do not want to talk to anyone.

Jo Beams comes across to me. She is an old acquaintance and we were at university together. Jo is always happy; even when she is complaining she seems happy. She gives me a hug and says she has to go and teach a singing class soon so will sit at the back for the meditation. I am feeling unsociable and our talk, such as it is, seems to take place in another space. We sit apart in our respective spaces. I hope I have not offended her with my lack of response. Meditation begins.

I have used a mantra for years but today it does not arise. I just sit with nothing. Sometimes my eyes are open, sometimes closed. I watch Gen Lama. He is a rock. His silence is strong and gentle. After five minutes a question comes into my mind: 'where is Gen Lama'? Then a series of images arise: I see myself stand up, take up a two-handed Samurai sword, approach Gen Lama while he meditates and bring the sword down on that brown shaven head, splitting it in two. Blood, brains and bone are exposed. I look into his head and ask, 'Where is Gen Lama?

Where do these images come from? Perhaps from Gen Lama, perhaps from a recent reading of an interview with a neurosurgeon who spoke of brains and consciousness. Who knows where they come from, but I am left with the insistent question, 'where is Gen Lama?' When the meditation period is over I leave, weeping. Perhaps I had some grief to trade after all. But these do not seem to be the tears of grief. They are the tears that come from being in the presence of, and merging with, a great soul. They are the tears of a weakening ego and perhaps that is my grief. Such tears leak away the ego's power so it begins to lose its strength and value. Breaking down the boundaries of the ego by weeping is an uncontrollable result of spiritual practice. Some years ago at my Guru's ashram in Kerala I remember weeping for days on end. I complained to one of the swamis about how lacking I was in self-control. He dismissed my complaint with a scoff and told me I should be thankful for such a gift.

Three days after the meditation session with the Gyuto Monks I return for another session. After the 12 o' clock meditation program there is question time where I ask Gen Lama: 'I can see Gen Lama's body, but where is Gen Lama?' He replies in a soft voice, in the same manner in which he replies to each and every question put to him.

Finally the translation comes from Sonam: 'a long time ago there was a radical monk with psychic powers who lived at the time of the fifth Dalai Lama. The fifth Dalai Lama had been very successful at developing his kingdom but had, at some point, decided he would go into a cave and meditate. When someone asked the radical monk where the Dalai Lama was he said he was in the town looking at rich brocades. This was considered to be an insult to the Dalai Lama so they arrested the radical monk. When the Dalai Lama finally heard of this he said that the radical monk was correct for while he had been meditating in the cave he had been thinking of the brocades in the town'.

Gen Lama then said he hoped I was not the reincarnated radical monk for he had wanted to look at the shops in Hobart after this tour. He then said that on a deeper level he does not know who he is or where he is and if he did know this he would be enlightened. On the face of it his answer did not seem to be an answer at all, yet it was deeply satisfying. He had not directly answered my question, yet he had left me with a sense of connection and profundity. How was this possible? What meaning had passed between us that had not been framed and encapsulated by the words he used but had left me wordlessly gratified?

The question I asked of Gen Lama has persisted, while his reply seems to have a potency that drives me to ask again: where am I and who am I? Yet if Gen Lama cannot tell me where he is, how am I, a worldly westerner to know where or who *I am*?

Certainly the words Gen Lama used gave me the opportunity to answer this question in my own way, which is perhaps what he intended. In addition, his words can be interpreted in several ways. When he referred to looking in shop windows, he implied that we are where our thoughts are. Yet while I know we are not our thoughts – we *have* thoughts – it seemed to me he was also saying something important about a quality of being that comes when our thoughts have focus and are strong. And while saying he was not enlightened, it is doubtful if any enlightened soul would say he is such, so the question of his state of grace was left open.

The question of where or who I am is a spiritual one but it wears empirical clothing. To be 'somewhere' implies that we are in a place that has a relatively precise location in space and time. This kind of empirical precision is demanded by a culture that relies on explicit details and the expectation that everything will have a visible, precise and differential location. The culture that has these expectations comes supported by the language of classical mechanical science. The material world that can be mapped by this kind of language was called by the theoretical physicist David Bohm, the explicate order.[2] This is the order of the everyday physical universe, which contains a multiplicity of physical forms. This visible world of material objects is reflected in, and reinforced by, the language of materialism, which has a bias towards the precise location and differential measurement of objects. In this explicit world there can be a relatively precise answer to where a thing is, as for example the question: 'Where is my book?' Answer: 'It's on the third shelf, four books from the left hand end'.

Bohm called the other great order of the universe the implicate order. This is often considered to be a mysterious order and has been much ignored by Bohm's fellow scientists. Within the implicate order there are no visible, extended and differential relations in time or space. In this domain there is no possibility

Trekking the Big Picture

of arriving at even a moderately precise location in time and space in response to such questions as 'where is Gen Lama?' This kind of question relates not to measurements in space and time but to the essence of Gen Lama's being and the essence of being has no precise or explicit location. Ambiguity of being exists because being is an event beyond time and space; it is part of Bohm's implicate order. It seems to me that Gen Lama's answer to my question was pointing me towards the natural ambiguity of being and the context of the implicate order.

The philosophy of being was a central concern for European philosophers in the twentieth century. On my bookshelf there is a book I have had for thirty years called *Being and Time*. The German philosopher Martin Heidegger wrote it. Throughout his long career Heidegger was preoccupied with the question of the meaning of being. For Heidegger, the central question of philosophy was 'what does being mean?' He felt that in general Western philosophy had forgotten about being and there was a need to restate its central importance. He set out to do this by concentrating on the being of humans, which he called *Dasein*. I do not intend to re-interpret or criticize Heidegger's philosophy here, except to say that I believe he asked the wrong question. The question he should have asked was not 'what does being mean?' but the prior question, 'what does meaning mean?' or, more precisely, 'what is the meaning of meaning?'

This is the question we need to ask in order to answer Heidegger's original question because the answer to the nature of being arises out of the earlier question of the meaning of meaning. I am therefore suggesting that being is actually an aspect of meaning. In other words, there is nothing more to being than what can be understood about the nature of meaning. From this position (being as meaning) the question of being's constitution (what and who am I) can only be satisfactorily answered by addressing what Heidegger and all other western philosophers have taken for granted, or neglected for so many years, and that is the nature of 'meaning' *per se*. So the first question we need to ask about being, is: what is meaning?

Questions about being are essentially spiritual journeys, and a spiritual journey needs to have a definite beginning. On this journey the most important decision we can make is to decide where to begin. If we begin some way into the journey then our view will be narrowed and a lot of things will have to be assumed and taken for granted on the way. This is what happened to the French philosopher Rene Descartes (1596–1650). He began not at the beginning but well into his journey, i.e. at the point of saying: 'I think therefore I am'. He could well have said: 'I sleep therefore I am', or 'I garden therefore I am'. As a consequence of this 'down-the-track' beginning his philosophy developed into a split between head and heart, mind and body, and what has become known as the divide between the subjective and the objective.

I am suggesting here that with questions of being we should begin with the biggest picture possible so that nothing is assumed, taken for granted or left out. The only beginning that fulfils these requirements is to focus on the question of meaning. How do we know that meaning is really the priority, first-order beginning? Well we know that meaning is the ground of everything because it is impossible to escape or step outside it. There is no outside of meaning. Here is a small experiment: just for a moment try to not make any meaning. I suggest that in this attempt you will fail because trying not to make meaning is a sure way to make some. Even when you say, 'my world is futile, absurd and meaningless' you create the meaning associated with these ideas. And if we are silent and do not speak at all, our bodily movements create non-verbal meaning. While you may not yet be convinced by the case for the absolute inclusiveness of meaning, the thesis of this big-picture trek that I present here is that we live through and within a universal ocean of meaning. This view translates into the statement that my being is meaning and the being of beings – God – is meaning. From this position I can say that in the beginning was meaning, and meaning is my being and meaning is God – the being of beings. It is therefore, possible to know that I exist and that God exists because it is not possible to live without meaning.

Even though for centuries Western philosophers have veiled the subject of meaning in the darkness of forgetting we nevertheless are capable of gaining a purchase on this *fundamentum absolutum;* the fundamental ground of everything mental and physical. Gaining a purchase on meaning represents the science of the underlay, for meaning is the underlay for every discourse whether religious or scientific. Such discourses are written down in the form of myths, legends, books, papers and documents: the *Holy Bible* for Christians and Jews, the *Quran* for Muslims, the *Upanishads* and the *Bhagavad Gita* for Hindus, and so on. A similar mode of expression operates for science. For example, we have the books, papers and journals of classical mechanics and those of quantum mechanics.

The much neglected science of meaning thus underlies every religious practice and scripture and also every scientific paper, method and experiment. A study of meaning represents the place we should begin in our studies of any and all religious beliefs systems as well as the place to begin training in any aspect of science; hence it is the place to begin our inner spiritual trek into this exploration of being. To study meaning is truly an interdisciplinary experience. However, to study meaning is not to study a body of knowledge opposed to science or religion as it does not dispute the legitimacy of these great traditions. Rather, the study of meaning is the large study of the underpinning of all specialized knowledge. It is a general study that strengthens, deepens and enlarges our understanding of our chosen and more specialized field of interest.

The enlargement and increased depth of profundity that comes with the study of meaning happens because meaning is always implicitly present within whatever it is we study, whether that is religion, science or a skills training needed for a vocation. The science of meaning is, therefore, not a secret or different kind of knowledge for it is always present within every discourse and every activity. It should, however, be acknowledged that a broad, tolerant and profound world-view does challenge the limited views and literal understandings of fundamentalists, whether they are religious or scientific.

The challenge posed by a deeper understanding is perhaps most pointed in relation to materialism and the other associated 'isms' of naturalism, realism and positivism.[3] As we shall see on this trek through meaning, the narrowness and superficiality of materialism comes about because it ignores or denies any role to meaning. By the use of this simple parsimony scientific materialism can justify itself while condemning as delusional belief in God. Perhaps with a similar limited gaze consumers can believe that redemption can come from shopping. Thus the increase in profundity that comes from the study of meaning challenges no specialized field of knowledge, but it does contest narrow and superficial views, judgments and opinions that are often based on dogma, prejudice or ignorance.

* * *

For many poets and philosophers the creative principle of *imagination* is considered to be the supreme faculty rather than meaning. This has been the tradition for philosophers such as Owen Barfield, (1898–1997) and a raft of romantic poets like William Blake (1757–1827) and more recently Kathleen Raine (1908–2003). Blake refers to the imagination as 'the Human Existence Itself',[4] while for Kathleen Raine: 'Our world is real because it is the creation of the human imagination'.[5] However, for the early Greek philosophers the supreme faculty was *nous* or intellect rather than imagination. *Nous* was seen to be the faculty of comprehension or understanding, which relates to how we can make sense of what we see, hear, taste or feel. As to what constitutes *nous* various terms like sense perception and reason were applied but these failed to explain the nature of *nous*. Many of the ancient philosophers saw our ability to understand to be a given that came from the eternal cosmic mind. Now the relationship between our human ability to understand and the divine cosmic mind held true for Blake and the romantics, however, they emphasized the creative principle of mind and spoke of the eternal world as the world of the imagination. Thus the realm of mind, involving both the human faculty of comprehension together with the divine cosmic mind has been traditionally described using the terms *imagination* or intellect (*nous*).

I am more a cartographer than a poet so maybe this is the reason why I have difficulties with the idea that the creative principle of imagination is the supreme faculty of mind. In addition, I do not think that explaining the ancient problem of how it is we understand (*nous*) is well served by reference to sense perceptions, intellect or reason. The use of these traditional terms carries so much historical baggage that any discussion based on them does not probe the semantic tendrils of our ability to comprehend. Thus while I do not wish to argue with the poetic idea of the imagination as the supreme faculty, for there is much to agree with the poetry of this interpretation, I also do not want to re-tread the over-used paths of the philosophy of mind.

The use of various terms like, 'imagination, 'nous' or 'meaning' represent attempts to map the territory of mind. It seems to the mapmaker in me that *meaning* is a by far the superior term in which to discuss mind and/or our supreme ability to understand rather than applying either 'imagination' or 'intellect' (*nous*) as fulcrum terms. The word, 'meaning' already implies an ability to understand and comprehend so any discussion of the conditions and laws of meaning will automatically involve the human condition of understanding. In plotting the hidden contours of meaning much of what has been said by ancient philosophers as well as the poets of the imagination will be brought into relief and seen, within the big picture context, to be true. Therefore, it is to meaning rather than the imagination or intellect, which I now turn to survey. The non-physical territory to be surveyed, however, is entirely different from that of land or coastline and so the precise magnetic points of north and south, east and west are of no use at all in this endeavor. As a consequence, we cannot take a GPS reading of the conditions of meaning; they do not have a latitude or longitude and nor is meaning solid and neither is it visible. Where then do we begin with our topographic map of meaning?

We can begin to gain a purchase on the territory of meaning by examining its two states. To begin with we can refer to meaning as the ultimate *sine qua non*; as a universal and divine quintessence or as the *fundamentum absolutum*. As this trek is through the big picture of meaning I choose to speak of this primary state as the meaning of Meaning. I use a capital 'M' to denote a sense of the absolute. It is this large and absolute sense that is missing from all linguistic and semiotic analyses for these disciplines tend to concentrate on meaning's secondary state or function. We can speak of Meaning's secondary function as the meaning of everything **other** than Meaning. This secondary sense is the meaning we humans make by thinking, using language, signs and expressions and by physical activity. This secondary sense is signified by the concept of the 'relative', and of 'process', and is denoted by the use of a lower case 'm'.

We can say that the difference between the meaning *of* something and the meaning of Meaning is seen in the difference between being and becoming. Being is the given, unchangeable and quintessential state of the meaning of Meaning, while becoming represents the changes and transformations that result from making sense of the world through the learning processes associated with maturation and development. While these two senses (being and becoming) are distinct, they are interconnected and indeed integrated. Their integration means that the divine is linked implicitly to the human; that the being of every particular individual can make sense (meaning) of the world in a variety of ways throughout her or his life. By these actions an individual changes by and through using the medium that has already been given by the being of beings – the meaning of Meaning – God.

How else are we to speak about Meaning? In addition to the two states of meaning there are two codes that are involved with the meaning we make. These are the codes of implicit and explicit meaning. The codes of implicit meaning are always hidden from view. This kind of relative meaning is contained within the implications and contexts that surround every visible, explicit and differential message, saying or sign. Implicit codes contain the potentials that are yet-to-be made manifest while the explicit codes of meaning always involves manifest, actual, differential and kinetic forms that move in space and can be measured or represented in language.

Meaning is not like a log of wood so we are unable to speak of it in terms of any measurement or computation. As we shall see, the meaning of Meaning has a fullness, a cosmic plenum; an implicit presence that is everywhere and at all times. To speak about this fullness presents the writer with some difficulties; however, in different contexts this fullness of Meaning can be illuminated in various ways. In other words, we can speak about Meaning as having a variety of 'aspects' or 'faces' through which its natural luminosity shines.

What are some of the aspects of Meaning? The first one to emphasize is **mind**. Mind is made up entirely of meaning and Meaning. The ordinary mind of humans therefore has a hidden aspect as well as a visible aspect. The hidden mind is made up of implicit meaning while the visible mind is constructed of explicit meaning. Every symbolic exchange that we make conveys both implicit and explicit meaning. In addition, every exchange of meaning, whether symbolic or not involves exchanges of intelligence and as a consequence every exchange represents a mental state or a state of mind that has both hidden and visible aspects.

In relation to the state of mind of the meaning of Meaning, this state represents a universal mind, and sometimes the phrase 'cosmic consciousness' is used to describe this state. This 'face' of Meaning, is therefore, the face of One cosmic mind that is everywhere and at all times implicitly present. We must remember, however, that the light of Meaning is not the light of the sun. The luminosity of Meaning is prior to the light of the sun and is exemplified by the sight within the mechanics of seeing: it is the light that enables the ordinary mind to have insight, realization and understanding. This is the divine light that gives us **vision** and this term describes yet another face of Meaning.

Another aspect of Meaning is **life**. But what is life? In his 1907 influential book, *Creative Evolution* Henri Bergeson used the term élan vital to describe the flux of life that he suggested we are able intuitively to experience through the flowing sequences of events.[6] 'Life' is usually thought of as a limited biological term that is now mostly used in relation to various life forms. Bergeson's concept of élan vital was so criticized by early twentieth century rationalists that it is almost never used in science today. Yet this term equates with the concept of *'life per se'*, which means that there is an important distinction here that has largely been lost. This is the distinction between *'life per se'* and 'life forms'. By losing this distinction we have tended to confuse the two meanings and, as a consequence, created further confusion by asking such questions as, 'when does life begin?

This is a wrong-headed question. Life *per se* has no beginning. It exists in the same way that the meaning of Meaning has no beginning for these are eternal and omnipresent organizational forces. Thus when we wish to speak of the fullness of

Meaning in terms of its creative organizational force we use the term 'life'. Hence, the creativeness of Meaning manifests in the order and organization of all life forms, in their birth, growth, development and death. These are the organizational patterns that order the life of every organism as well as creating the transience of every object.

Another aspect of Meaning is **spirit**. Spirit is the central concept of most religions. The idea of spirit represents an essential, vivifying, subtle energy often referred to in the Bible as the Holy Spirit or Holy Ghost. The Gospel of Mark, for example, tells how Jesus will baptize you with *pneuma* – the Greek term for Holy Spirit. John who baptizes with water said, in reference to Jesus, 'he shall baptize you with the Holy Ghost'. In other words, he will immerse you in the Spirit of Meaning so your life will be changed and be more meaningful.

In *The Existential Jesus*, John Carroll draws our attention to the traditional translation of the Greek – *pneuma hagion* – as 'Holy Spirit' or 'Holy Ghost'. Carroll says that in the original Greek, *pneuma* is not capitalized and that the Church's preference for this tends to erase the word's association with *wind, breath* and *spirit*.[7] The capitalized title of the 'Holy Spirit' also tends to give Meaning a personality and, in this restrictive sense, redirects our attention away from its dynamic fullness and omnipresence onto a restricted and objectified subject.

The last two 'faces' of Meaning to be mentioned here are **joy** and **love**. These are the feelings we experience when we open ourselves directly to Meaning. I will have more to say about these feelings in later Chapters. When combined together these various aspects of Meaning represent the numinous energy of *meaning-mind-life-spirit-vision-joy-love* or, simply, Meaning. The combination of these terms provides the writer with a basic vocabulary for describing and focusing in on a particular aspect, nuance or context of meaning, or Meaning. When attempting to paint the outlines of Meaning's fullness we need a vocabulary such as this. With these six aspects of Meaning, together with the states of becoming and being along with the qualities of implicit and explicit meaning we have the beginnings of a tool kit for exploring the territory of the big picture.

* * *

A further feature of Meaning involves the creation of our worldview or gaze. Every time we express ourselves in some way, either in thought or deed, we make meaning, and every meaning we make carries with it its own theory of meaning. We are generally unaware of the theory we use but it comes automatically with the manner in which we think, act and use symbols and signs. Our theory of meaning creates our worldview or gaze. In general, our gaze will come from the tendency to favor either division (explicit meaning) or unity (implicit meaning). When we favor the meanings of divisions and separations our gaze will be explicit and limited and our body tense. When we create meanings that connect, unify and which value implicitness our worldview will be big and our body relaxed. Between these extremes lies a mixture of ways of making meaning that depend upon our desires, rational explanations and feelings of empathy. With each way we make meaning there is an accompanying perspective as well as a bodily response.

People like the philosopher Descartes, who value explicit division, tend to see their world full of splits and gaps. They will say such things as, 'there is a split between mind and matter, or between rich and poor, or between black and white, or between Christians and Muslims, or between God and his creation,' which, by implication can never be filled. Others may say such things as, 'death is the negation of life', or 'I am a separate and independent person who has a solo mind and who is separate from society, the environment and God'. Some scientists even hold to the idea that there are multiple universes *out there*.

These contemporary and stressful ways of making meaning are the drivers of the 'isms' of materialism, positivism, rationalism and realism.

In contrast to those who see splits and divisions throughout the universe there are those optimists who make integrated meaning by stressing implicit connections and thus have a big-picture, unified world-view. This big picture view is built on the idea of a singular interconnected universe that has no splits, gaps or divisions within its holistic fabric. The integrated gaze reflects this current theory of Meaning and which locates humans as participants within a participatory universe. A participatory universe is an interconnected singular one in which every form and organism has a place and role to play and where each part is dependent on its neighbors and as well, on the underlying interconnecting fabric of Meaning. The making of integrated meaning is broadly reflected in the works of the European romantic poets as well as in the main teachings of Plato and in the ancient spiritual philosophy of *The Upanishads*. I should also add that the big-picture theory of Meaning differs from the conventional and limited linguistic view of meaning, which values separations and divisions and does not take into account the permanent underlay of the meaning of Meaning.

Some readers will also perceive that I am using the term 'Meaning' in a similar manner to the way 'Logos' was understood by the early Greek and Hebrew philosophers. In Greek philosophy, Logos refers to the order and organizational force of the cosmos. I argue that order and organization are both features of Meaning. In both Greek and Hebrew metaphysics the Logos was seen as the unifying principle of the cosmos. The central idea of this understanding was that the Logos links God to man in a singular monist system. This is also the central idea of the big-picture theory of Meaning presented here, a theory of absolute interconnection in which everything in the universe is linked into a singular monist consciousness.

The Stoics also believed there was only one Logos in the universe, one that was also present in every human. A similar view was held by the Chinese sage Lao Tzu who, as a contemporary of the Stoics, observed some 2000 years ago that,

> The world and its particles are not separate, isolated things but rather, one small particle contains the nature of the world just as the world contains the nature of each small particle; the nature of each is the same. The apparently single event is but a variation and segment of the great whole and the great whole is the combination of all single events. Thus, the single events contain the life experience of the whole.[8]

A contemporary view of this holistic relationship between meaning and Meaning – Dasein and the *fundamentum absolutum*, the individual and God – is a view that uses the interpreting device of the hologram. As an explanatory tool the hologram can help us to understand how each individual is an integrated part of the fabric of our collective and cosmic consciousness.

A hologram is a three-dimensional image that has been imprinted on to a photographic plate. When a laser beam illuminates the plate it reveals the three-dimensional image, almost identical to the original object. When a small region of the plate is cut off and is illuminated again by a laser beam, what we see is not a piece of the image but the whole image. This is extraordinary. It means that the whole of the three-dimensional image has been recorded in every part of the plate.

The whole is therefore replicated in every point on the plate while at the same time every point has contributed to the creation of the whole image. This exchange symmetry – of part-to-whole and whole-to-part – gives the hologram its undivided interconnectedness or wholeness and represents a general explanation for how multiplicity is unified. If we see the consciousness of the

Logos as a hologram, then individual minds will represent various external points on the whole fabric of cosmic consciousness so that each individual becomes a small prism through which the larger (whole) of heaven shines. Individual minds thereby represent local flashpoints in the divine ferment of the Logos.

Swami Vivekananda penned something similar when writing to a friend on the 3rd March 1894 he said:

> We believe every being is divine, is God. Every soul is a sun covered with clouds of ignorance, the difference between soul and soul is due to the difference in density of these layers of clouds ... We believe that this is the very essence of the Vedas.[9]

And my own spiritual teacher, Amma speaks about this as one Reality: 'there is one truth that shines through all of creation. Rivers and mountains, plants and animals, the sun, the moon and the stars, you and I – all are expressions of this one Reality.'[10]

Our holographic relationship to this one Reality can be liken to a dynamic fractal. A fractal is a geometric pattern displaying self-similarity in that small details of its structure viewed at any scale (large or small) repeat elements of the overall pattern. The whole pattern is therefore contained in each part while each part also replicates the patterning of the whole. In this holographic or fractal sense, each of us contributes to the collective cosmic mind of the universe, while at the same time the patterns of heaven are reflected in and through each of us. This is what the sage Lao Tzu was saying.

If we are able to appreciate our holographic relationship to the Logos we will be engaged in a process where relative meaning recognizes its own essence. This is the recognition of our *Divine Humanity*; a term Kathleen Raine tells us was used by both the Swedish philosopher and scientist, Emanuel Swedenborg

(1688–1772) as well as the poet, William Blake to refer to the human condition.[11] In terms of Meaning, our Divine Humanity constitutes a multilayered vision, one in which the distinctions of the vision (of part-to-whole and whole-to-part) are not some personal poetic fancy, but spring from the actual multilayered conditions of Meaning *per se*. It goes without saying, that this kind of multilayered seeing is spiritual.

A holographic understanding of who I am carries with it an appreciation of the uniqueness, integrity and divinity of each individual mind. It also carries an understanding of how this communal diversity of minds is vitally necessary to make up the interconnected whole patterned fabric of every society. Such a holographic view is also important for cultural and environmental contexts for when cultural and ecological diversity are devalued, health and wellbeing are reduced. Similarly, when scientific, economic or religious intolerance begin to exclude differences of opinion there is social sickness rather than a healthy unified diversity that informs a coherently attuned community context.

The process of recognizing our holographic relationship to the whole of Meaning (the Logos) is a learning process of becoming aware of our Divine Humanity. This ancient yet modern view suggests that the question that I asked Gen Lama is one that begins the process of unravelling the hologram of our being.

Chapter 2 – The heavenly peaks

One frosty morning when I was eight years old something happened that suddenly changed my view of the world. It was as if a curtain had been drawn back and I could see a magical, spiritual dimension beyond the mundane of the everyday. This realization came with a great deal of pain.

It happened this way. We lived on a farm high in the mountains of northeast Tasmania. One morning I went out by myself to set rabbit traps. It was the first time I had gone trapping on my own without Michael, my elder brother. Michael usually came along to set the traps. Setting steel traps is a difficult exercise for an eight year old. On this particular morning it was very frosty and I had to kneel down in the frosty grass while putting my foot on the steel spring of the trap and then slowly insert my cold fingers under the jaws to lift the tongue to set the trap.

Once I had managed this I laid the trap in a prepared hole in the mouth of a rabbit burrow and then began to cover it gently with fine dirt. I was leaning over, looking down on the trap and dropping dirt on the tongue when suddenly it went off catching my thumb in its steel jaws and throwing dirt up into my face. I was totally blinded and in horrendous pain. I let out a terrible cry and kept on yelling, overcome by fear of being blind as well the excruciating pain in my hand. Finally I managed to step on the spring of the trap and pull my hand free. I lay down on the cold grass crying loudly and as a consequence my vision started to return as the tears began to wash the dirt from my eyes.

This trauma suddenly ended, however, because just as I began to see again I heard a voice calling my name from the hill above. I thought it must be my mother come to look for me. I stopped crying, jumped to my feet and ran up the paddock, over the fence and through the bracken fern to the top of the hill. No one was there. I was about a kilometer from home so I set off as fast as I could and reached the back door to find my mother in the laundry hard at work washing clothes in the old copper. Showing her my mangled thumb I asked if she had called out to me down the paddock. 'No,' she replied.

Further questioning only got me the brusque reply that she had not left the house all morning. While she bandaged my thumb I told her I heard a voice calling my name when I was lying on the ground crying after catching my thumb in the rabbit trap. We were a practical farming family who never spoke about things that might embarrass, like mental illness, so my mother dealt with this odd outburst by asking if I had not imagined it. I knew her question signaled the end to any discussion about celestial voices calling me. Unlike my mother, I felt pleased about this mysterious event. It left me with the feeling that a magical someone or something was looking out for me.

This event gave me hope that there was more to my life than the terror of school with its hard-edged moral rectitude and its military-type discipline for bad spelling. Hearing a heavenly voice call my name was a secret joy that had stopped my pain and fear and introduced me to a new way of seeing beyond the everyday. But where had the voice come from? As I have never heard 'voices' again the probability that I had a childhood psychotic episode is low. In any case I felt then as well as now that I was not psychotic, however, the voice was real and it had come from somewhere. My conclusion now is that it came from what I would call a celestial manifestation of the meaning of Meaning: my true self. This is not the imagination, which is part of the ordinary mind. The true self is a feature of our cosmic mind.

A sympathetic psychologist would no doubt say that my voice-hearing episode was a common occurrence and that at times of high stress the mind can play all kinds of tricks. This response is like my mother suggesting that it was my imagination. These are typical rational reactions that try and make us feel comfortable with the current mainstream view that erases the context of Meaning from any discussion or analysis. The sympathetic psychologist might even liken my episode to those occasions when someone who has recently lost a close relative unexpectedly has a vision of that person. Again, this is said to be a common occurrence, which is usually interpreted as simply the ordinary mind so badly wanting to see the close relative that it conjures up the vision. Yet another view of such events is that these kinds of visions are special features of a spiritual seeing; a seeing that comes from the underlying domain of Meaning.

The rational and psychological interpretation of such experiences as these would become more credible if the subject matter of Meaning formed part of their standard analysis. This is generally not the case as Meaning is simply deleted from any consideration and hence, the possible causes of unusual phenomena are easily reduced to 'the mind is playing tricks'. However, even when one is sympathetic to the possibility of hearing celestial voices or seeing visions it is difficult to make sense of these manifestations without some understanding of Meaning.

When I was eight and heard my name called from the hill above I did not immediately know my true self, but from that signpost event came the potential for developing a spiritual intelligence. This potential was deepened and made actual many years later by my guru, Mata Amritanandamayi, or Amma for short.

I first met Amma in Sydney in 1992 and a year later had my fist hug. When Amma took hold of me she pushed my head into her shoulder and held me tight. I do not remember if anything was said. All I remember was the feeling. This was a baptism by *pneuma*, the kind Jesus used to give. Outside the hall I lay down under a gum tree, disoriented. I looked up at the midday sky and literally saw stars. I felt such strange happiness. I did not know what to do with it but I was sure it would pass. Amma's cosmic pull had opened and widened the doors of perceptions into the cosmos of Meaning. This was my second experience of our One holographic consciousness. But how do we speak about the One consciousness?

In Chinese philosophy one of the oldest ideas is that of Tao, which is conventionally translated as The Way. According to C.G. Jung in his book on *Synchronicity* Richard Wilhelm translated the Tao as 'meaning'. The following translation of the *Tao Te Ching*, (Chapter 25) is recorded by Jung in the following poetic manner:

> *There is something formless yet complete.*
> *That existed before heaven and earth.*
> *How still! How empty!*
> *Dependent on nothing, unchanging,*
> *All pervading, unfailing,*
> *One may think of it as the mother of all things under heaven.*
> *I do not know its name*
> *But I call it 'meaning'.*
> *If I had to give it a name, I would call it 'The Great'.*[1]

So now let us turn to three holistic principles of Meaning in order to understand more about it and to note that these three principles imply a universal order. This is an order that includes all aspects of nature, whether organic or inorganic, mental and physical. 'Order' is often set against the ideas of 'randomness,' 'chance' or 'chaos'. Randomness and chance have become important ideas for determining statistical probabilities in all kinds of scientific experiments, yet these experimental values do not provide us with a safe basis for big picture judgments, even though many scientists believe the universe is random and that chance represents the gold standard for measurements. As Meaning is normally erased from any scientific theory or experiment the idea that the universe has an underlying order is either considered to be inexplicable or wrong. Yet when we include Meaning in our analyses of the world, 'order' automatically becomes an organizational condition of it.

The three principles of Meaning I want to discuss are: *interconnection, circularity,* and *omnipotence*. Together these three represent generic principles of nature and as a consequence, they assume the status of natural laws that order the universe.

The first law of Meaning is *interconnection*. This law refers to the existence of infinite interconnections throughout the universe. Interconnection is not a new idea for it is contained within the Taoist idea of The Way as well as early Greek thought about the nature of the cosmos. More recently the theoretical physicists David Bohm and Basil Hiley refer to this kind of interconnectedness in their book, *The Undivided Universe*.[2] In terms of Meaning, *interconnection* refers to the connections and links of relationships and in this regard the codes of implicit and explicit meaning are relevant. But first, let us look at the role of relations.

A focus on relations provides an answer to the 'what' of *interconnection* for relations connect and thus they constitute interconnections. Relations also give us a positive manner of speaking for relations tend to highlight links and integrations. When using the term *'relations'* I am not only referring to interpersonal exchanges or those involving love, but more generally to any link, connection or exchange between two or more explicit forms or objects. Readers should also note here I am suggesting that relations are essentially mental structures; they are the stuff of which the mind is made. Relations constitute the 'software' structures of the ordinary mind as well as the cosmic mind of Meaning. As mental structures relations exist as *relations of*

Meaning and as a consequence, every field of relations is a field of Meaning. Relations are therefore, not physical structures but organizational features that regulate the physical universe through the interactions of gravitational, electromagnetic, massless and scalar fields. Relations also organize the ordinary mind involving perceptions, conceptions, symbols, habitual behavior and the biological systems of the body.

Relations also exist within physical exchanges and interactions'. Hence, relations exist as the universal mental matrix encompassing the whole undivided universe. The image that comes from a system of infinite interconnections is the image of One-ness: a unified, singular whole in which there are no splits or divisions within its relational fabric. Within this holistic unity the physical world is not separate from the mental world as the physical world is always organized, regulated and structured by relations and in addition, both worlds are constructed from the same relational architecture of Meaning.

Scientists have known for a long time that every particle as well as every galaxy exists as a field of relations within larger fields of relationships. The physicist Henry Stapp who is well known for his work in quantum physics wrote that, 'an elementary particle is not an independently existing, un-analyzable entity. It is, in essence, a set of relationships that reach outward to other things.'[3] An outward reaching relationship implies intelligence and this intelligence can be demonstrated in the ability of relationships to create organized forms that interact in organized and regulated ways. A form can be solid, liquid, gaseous, abstract or symbolic. As is known, a form of any kind is an expression of a certain regular pattern or assembly of relations. Certain assemblies of relations create solid and concrete states of matter while other assemblies create the abstract forms of culture and symbols.

By using the vocabulary of relations it can be demonstrated that the universe is essentially a mental event since relations are mental structures. In addition, because relations are mental they have the same kind of creative and causal qualities as the cosmic whole of Meaning. This means that relations are *alive* and inherent within them are the capacities for *vision, joy* and *love*, which we humans can experience first hand. The first Law of *interconnection* thus confirms the underlying purpose of humanity, which is to love.

Relations operate as the social and propagating intelligent forces within every form, field and cosmic system in the universe. When we understand that relations have this kind of animate causality they assume the significant role of the self-propagating, intelligent agencies that can construct and structure the entire universe.

In terms of Meaning, there are three important and basic relations that construct the architecture of the universe. These are the relations of symmetry, non-symmetry and asymmetry. These three sets of relations are not isolated or separated from each other but form a unified continuum that constructs both the local, ordinary minds of individuals as well as the infinite and eternal mind of Meaning. The local and ordinary minds of individuals are largely constructed from the relations of asymmetry and non-symmetry while symmetry is the essential feature of the cosmic mind and as well, the underlying feature of ordinary minds.

Symmetry is a difficult concept to grasp at the outset and this is because it is essentially a non-ordinary mind state. Its essential quality is nameless. Dictionary definitions of 'symmetry' tend to construct it as an ordinary mind state, that is, as a passive by-product that is somehow associated with similar times, shapes, sizes or forms. Yet symmetry is much more than an interesting kind of similarity or isomorphism. It represents the essential character and quality of Meaning and hence, its potentials represent the animate and omnipotent creative forces that connect, construct, order and regulate each and every form in the universe.

Strictly speaking, symmetry is not so much a relationship as a potential relationship. Arising from the potentials of symmetry are the connections involving the relations of asymmetry and non-symmetry, or what can be called differences and systems. Differences and systems exist within the ordinary mind as explicit relations, in contrast to the implicit potentials of symmetry that exist within the cosmic mind of Meaning. This suggests there are no explicit meanings within the interconnections of the cosmic mind and there are, therefore, no 'relationships' that are explicit.

The symmetry potentials of the cosmic mind of Meaning exist and operate prior to the explicit relationships of time and space and the distinctions that are made by conscious deliberation. Symmetry is more the timeless potential for connect-ability than an established relationship within the ordinary mind of time and space. Symmetry represents the essential and implicit quality of the meaning of Meaning: the numinous essence of the Logos out of which the visible, physical world was, and continues to be born.

Symmetry potentials are 'non-local' potentials. The term *'non-local'* is used in science to mean the negative of locality. However, what is always missing from this scientific vocabulary about 'locality' or 'non-locality' is any reference to mind and thus to Meaning. These deletions do not operate here and as a consequence, any use of 'locality' refers to the activities and conditions of the ordinary mind of time and space. Such activities always have a location, that is, a detailed and differential position in time and space.

In terms of Meaning, the negative term *'non-local'* has the positive features of meaningful, intelligent interconnections that underpin all the ordinary mind distinctions and differences within space and time. Non-local refers to infinite interconnectedness: a state in which everything in the universe is connected to everything else, all of the time. This manifests as a cosmic intelligence or consciousness that operates instantaneously across the entire universe. This is the idea of a Mind-at-large. The negative term '*non-locality*' can, therefore, represent a positive singular and quintessential force: a universal constant that holistically interconnects everything in the universe into One Mind-at-large. The flexible nature of this universal constant comes from the quality of its implicitness and its universal scope is captured by the idea of the One ambient ocean of cosmic consciousness. Essentially this means that such connections operate and exist prior to bodily functions. Lacking ordinary mind differentiation, such connections are, by definition, symmetrical, non-local and implicit.

An instantaneous connection is not to be confused with a connection related to speed or velocity. The theory that the space of the universe is full of energy moving at super-luminary speeds (many times faster than the speed of light) is a theory of an ordinary mind world and it does not fit cosmic, non-local and instantaneous connections. An instantaneous connection has no speed or velocity. It is, rather, a universal constant – a condition that is always and forever present within the universe.

Instantaneous, non-local animate connections represent the intelligent implicitness or 'mind-stuff' of the universe. One of the founders of quantum physics, Sir James Jeans once remarked that 'the universe begins to look more like a great thought than like a great machine' and Arthur Eddington, agreed that 'the stuff of the world is mind-stuff.'[4] I would add that the 'mind stuff' of the universe represent Meaning. We can conclude then that the well-established scientific evidence of non-local, instantaneous connections[5] represents scientific evidence of the One cosmic consciousness of Meaning.

This essentially spiritual realm of the non-local provides us with, among other things, our sense of the present: the eternal NOW. The eternal NOW of the present is a non-ordinary mind state even though it is present within the ordinary mind. It is the permanent – I should say the eternal – state of our cosmic mind. It is also the basis of our ordinary mind and so it is there beneath the surface activity of the ordinary mind all the time. We do not have to do anything to experience it except stop – stop trying, stop thinking, stop every strategy to be good, wealthy, famous or smart. While this is simple advice it is difficult for an ordinary mind that buzzes like a beehive to stop and be in the eternal no-time of NOW. It is difficult to be in the NOW because to do so the ordinary mind has to go against its habits of continual thinking. To break these habits of thought usually requires long years of practice in meditation.

Another way of approaching the instantaneous connections of NOW is to understand that this experience endows us with 'heart meaning': love. Loving another always involves a double meaning: i) the love inherent within Meaning's implicit connections (which could be called 'joy' or 'bliss'); and ii) our idiosyncratic feelings of affection and attraction for another. These two loves (the cosmic and mine) synchronize in all feelings of affection and desire. Yet even though these two loves cohere in all our feelings of love they are not equal or the same. When my loves dominates we often feel afraid of losing the other. Such feelings are associated with our sense that we are a separate self that has possessions. Such feelings, when strong, tend to cloud over the blissful, unconditional heart meaning that is the feeling-nature of Meaning's implicit interconnections.

The heart of Meaning (the Spirit Supreme) is, therefore, the connected bliss of implicitness in which everyone shares. This universal heart is usually experienced as if it were a separate and private feeling. Yet individual people do not have separate hearts (even though we do have separate heart organs). There is only one unified field of Meaning and therefore only on Supreme heart. We experience the connecting energy of this One heart when we merge in love with others or when we realize the joy of the NOW. When we realize this non-local heart energy it is both intimate yet impersonal for it is the connection of the universal Host that we are feeling.

It is common to confuse these feelings of love and think that the object of our affection has produced our intimate feelings and desires. This is not possible. It is the impersonal heart energy of interconnection that comes from within that provides the foundational drive for the relative agency of the more possessive and object-centered desires to flourish. The joyful implicitness of Meaning's interconnections transcends symbols, cultural styles and bodily sensations of pain and pleasure. These implicit relationships exist within everything and between everything, from the smallest mass-less particle to the furthest galaxy. They are always there for us to experience whenever we stop and realize the joy of NOW.

Thus the symmetry potentials of NOW represent a non-ordinary mind state; a state of mind prior to the asymmetrical and non-symmetrical relations that construct the ordinary mind. These two sets of relations represent the shape and extension that belong to physical objects as well as to the symbolic forms involved in all measurements. These two sets of relations also involve movement and change that register within the ordinary mind. This brings me to the ordinary mind character established by the relations of asymmetry and non-symmetry.

Asymmetrical relations establish ordered systems of irreversible relations while non-symmetry refers to our ability to draw distinctions and establish differences. Importantly, both these relations are secondary relations for they logically derived their relative agency from the infinite potentials of symmetry.

These two secondary and ordinary mind relations of asymmetry and non-symmetry order, structure and create the differential characteristics of space and time and they account for the multiple geometric extensions (*res extensia*) and the movement and shape of all physical forms throughout space and time. These derivative relations are inherent in all aspects of the physical world as well as within our mental acts of perception, conception and imagination. In brief, the relations of non-symmetry and asymmetry structure the many and varied processes of the local, ordinary mind of the individual as well as the movements and forms of the physical world.

In conclusion, the law of *interconnection* implies there is no outside of Meaning; its all-encompassing scope and interconnections are universal, absolute, infinite and eternal. This means there are no splits or separations in fabric of the universe. For example, there are no separations between objects and subjects, or between mind and matter. As a consequence of *interconnection* Meaning is logically everywhere: omnipresent. Everything is therefore interrelated, which also means that nothing is born, created, spoken of, measured or located in a space or a time that is outside the precincts of this singular all-embracing context.

From the first law of *interconnection* we can say that the unified single mind of the Numinous One has an interconnected structure that contains within it the ordinary minds of every individual. The relations of symmetry, non-symmetry and asymmetry constitute this interconnected structure of the cosmic and ordinary minds. This singular unifying structure of Meaning represents the undivided holographic holiness of our being.

The second law of Meaning is concerned with the shape of Meaning and follows on from the omnipresence of the first law. Meaning's all-encompassing interconnections are circular which gives us the idea of a singularity or One-ness. One-ness is a concept that implies circularity. Meaning's interconnections are circular in respect to the ordinary mind as well as our cosmic mind. For example, circularity can be seen in the planetary shapes that populate the universe. Circularity is a biological function within the processes called self-replication and self-organization. Circularity is also inherent within chaos theory as iteration and self-similarity. Circularity is also seen in the function of discourse as the tendency of language to refer back to itself. Ordinary mind circularity is created when we deliberately become involved in self-reflective thinking. On these occasions we tend to mirror, in a self-similar manner, the circularity inherent within the cosmic mind. This is why self-reflection can lead us closer to the Spirit Supreme.

Another ordering feature of the circularity of Meaning is the life cycle of birth, growth and death to which everything in the universe is subjected. The life cycle of birth, growth and death represents the circular order of all transient things. 'Things' represent the forms created within the ordinary mind so it is the ordinary mind that both deals in transient things and is, ultimately, itself transient. This circularity of the ordinary mind can be extended so that we can also begin to think of it as the evolution of consciousness.[6] The processes of a circular evolution of the ordinary mind may also be interpreted in the religious terms as reincarnation, as the belief that the soul can take many births before finally returning to the implicit and Divine context from which it began.

Yet another consequence of the second law of Meaning is that any linear sequences will always represent a partial picture within a larger implicit context, a context that will always refer back to the details of the sequence. This circularity indicates that within the universe there are no linear stand-alone sequences that have a beginning or an end. Within Meaning there are no beginnings or ends, only circular transformations or changes of meaning. To take some simple examples, death is often seen as an end, but in terms of Meaning this is incorrect. Death is simply a transformation, a change in the evolution of consciousness. Similarly, birth is not a beginning of life but a transformation of life that has gone before. To successfully argue against the circularity of Meaning one would have to demonstrate a stand-alone linear sequence that had a definite beginning or end and does not constitute a transformation. As no one to my knowledge has yet been able to demonstrate this we can safely assume that beginnings or ends do not exist, even for humans and hence, linear sequences are simply limited visions of the unlimited circularity of Meaning.

The circularity of the second law of Meaning also implies a gestalt. A gestalt has two exchange elements. These are: a set of explicit details, objects or parts that represent the transient and outer features of a more permanent background context. Thus, any object represents a part of an event; the part that is visible. The major part of an event is the invisible context and it is this part that involves an intelligent organization that represents the event as well as the broader cosmic context that gives rise to the event.

The big picture is always created through the circular exchange elements of this gestalt. Yet whenever we reduce ourselves by taking on a materialistic view we follow the same limiting perspective. This comes from a linear pattern of thought where we focus on specific, explicit details, objects or parts and then delete or erase the broader and deeper contexts from which these objects have arisen. In this manner we destroy the gestalt of Meaning and replace it with an illusion of a linear stand-alone causal sequence.

The circularity of the second law of Meaning implies there is no such thing as an individual object or set of objects existing on their own without an underlying ordering context. As an example, there is no such thing as a separate and solo mind or organism that has a capacity for self-organization. In terms of the second law of Meaning, the ordinary mind is simply the visible part of the cosmic event called Meaning.

The third law of Meaning is concerned with the ideas of priority, order and causality and how these come together as omnipotence. The third law indicates that Meaning is prior to everything else in the universe. This means it is prior to the matter and mass of the physical universe. The priority of Meaning logically occurs because the explicit forms of the universe are always secondary and derivative of the Meaning events that created them. While materialists assume that the physical objects of the universe have priority and causality, the theoretical physicist, David Bohm would have disagreed for he argued that the implicate order creates the explicate order of the physical world. I am agreeing here with Bohm's view but taking his theory further and saying that the implicate order represents the implicitness of Meaning, while the explicate order represents the explicit meaning that is associated with the physical forms of the universe.

The priority of Meaning also concerns the ideas of order and causality. The order of the universe is observed in the transient nature of all visible objects and forms. This order of transience means that every visible object has a birth or beginning, followed by a period of unfolding, and then by a period of enfolding until the visible form or object disappears back into the implicitness from whence it came. The order of these transformations – from birth, development/growth and death – provide the structure of a cycle consisting of asymmetrical and non-symmetrical relations. These relations are always secondary and they constitute the ordered transformations and shape of every transient object and form. These relations have not created the order of transience but that order has sprung from the prior and underlying implicit symmetrical potentials of Meaning.

Causality is implied by this order of transience and also by the priority of Meaning. The causal agency within objects is sourced from the domain that is prior to all other domains. This is Bohm's implicate order, or what I call the domain of symmetry potentials or the meaning of Meaning. The causal agency of Meaning has flexibility, openness and creativity. In other words, Meaning's laws write themselves; hence they are animate, self-sustaining, self-creating and self-organizing and can therefore be called uncaused causes.[7]

Ralph Waldo Emerson proposed the same kind of agency for

his Laws of the Soul. In the text of his 1838 Divinity School Address Emerson wrote that, 'these laws execute themselves. They are out of time, out of space, and not subject to circumstance.' Emerson went on to say that the Laws of the Soul make man 'Providence to himself'. This insightful phrase reflects both the universal scope as well as the circular nature of Meaning for it points to the manner in which our minds are interconnected with, and integrated into, the singular presence of our One cosmic mind.

The causality of Meaning comes from the symmetry potentials that organize the creation, development and destruction of all forms, from particles to people. Like Bohm's implicate order the biochemist, Rupert Sheldrake made use of this idea of a prior causal field when describing the creation of biological forms. Sheldrake called his prior causal field a 'morphic field'.[8] According to Sheldrake, a morphic field contains the organizing potentials for the creation, maintenance and development of all forms, which include the forms of molecules, crystals, cells, tissue, organisms and societies. Sheldrake does not, however, use the vocabulary of Meaning and therefore does not speak about mind, relations or implicitness, but he does speak about 'morphic resonance'.

According to Sheldrake, morphic resonance is the influence of *like upon like*. Sheldrake argues that a morphic field resonates with the effects of *like upon like* and also that this morphic resonance 'enables the regularities of nature to be understood as governed by habits inherited by morphic resonance'.[10] He suggests, for example, that the 'development of crystals is shaped by morphogenetic fields with an inherent memory of previous crystals of the same kind'. Sheldrake calls his hypothesis the hypothesis of formative causation. The vocabulary Sheldrake uses derives from biology while I tend to use a language of Meaning. The process of morphic resonance, of *like upon like* can well describe the process of *implicit to implicit* meaning exchanges (to be discussed in later chapters). What is exchanged in *like upon like* processes is an implicit like-ness that is iterated many times and which, for Sheldrake, are exchanges across generations. Sheldrake's morphic fields are therefore similar to Bohm's implicate order and to the cosmic context of Meaning.

The third law of Meaning indicates that the physical world is not composed of separate objects that affect each other through material causes, but, in Emerson's words, is the product of 'one will, of one mind; and that one mind is everywhere active, in each ray of the star, in each wavelet of the pool; and whatever opposes that will, is every-where balked and baffled, because things are made so, and not otherwise.' With these words Emerson describes the self-caused nature of the Providence within. From this position he is able to say that, 'good is positive. Evil is privative, not absolute.' Hence, the only absolute in the cosmos is Meaning, which as a self-sustaining and self-caused absolute is, by definition, *omnipotent*.

*	*	*

The three laws of Meaning: *interconnection, circularity* and *omnipotence* are closely associated with those principles in the West that have been traditionally attributed to God. Essentially, the three laws of Meaning provide an integrated cosmology that is more in tune with Plato teachings than with Aristotle. From the point of view of the three laws of Meaning, the all-knowing cosmic mind of God transcends nature yet at the same time is omnipresent and immanent within it.

The three laws of Meaning thus give a general outline to the hologram of our One cosmic consciousness and in the process they provide support for an integrated view of the cosmos, and as well provide a contemporary underpinning for the many texts written by such romantic poets as William Blake. The scope of these three laws embraces all those experiences of mystical and visionary presence we associate with a sense of Divinity as well as all the mundane meanings we make with our ordinary minds in our everyday lives. The ever-presence of Meaning, therefore, involves the mystical domain (hearing a voice call my name) as well as all the mundane time and space-based exchanges of the ordinary mind. In other words, empiricism and mysticism are interconnecting partners and not divorced as is commonly supposed.

* * *

To summarize the tools of Meaning found along the path of the last two chapters; firstly there are the two states of meaning and Meaning. The relative state of meaning involves the concepts of *process* and *becoming* and is denoted by the use of a lower case 'm'. In contrast, there is the infinite and absolute state of Meaning which refers to the ultimate *sine qua non*; the divine being, and which is denoted by a capital 'M'. There are also the interrelated codes of implicit and explicit meaning. These two codes relate to the states of meaning and Meaning in the following manner: the processes and relativities of meaning are always structured by both explicit and implicit meaning, while the infinite and eternal state of Meaning always contains the quality and symmetry potentials of implicitness.

David Bohm's categories of the implicate and explicate orders thus reflect the cardinal codes of implicit and explicit meaning. In addition to these conditions there are the three laws of Meaning: *interconnection, circularity, omnipotence*, which refer to the generic principles of Meaning. Finally, there are the various 'faces' that when combined together represent the numinous energy of *meaning-mind-life-spirit-vision-joy-love* or, simply, Meaning. These states, codes and principles now provide us with a tool kit with which to view how the relative mind of individuals connects with, and relates to, the cosmic One-ness of Meaning.

Chapter 3 – Climbing Blake's Pass

On the 22nd November 1802 the English painter, poet and engraver William Blake wrote a letter to Thomas Butt, his publisher in London. Blake was living with his wife in a cottage in Sussex and under the countryside's mild influence was rediscovering the power and joy of nature. The letter to Butt was in the form of a poem. One of the verses speaks of a fourfold vision:

> *Now I a fourfold vision see*
> *And a fourfold vision is given to me*
> *Tis fourfold in my supreme delight*
> *And three fold in soft Beulah's night*
> *And twofold Always.*
> *May God us keep*
> *From single vision & Newton's sleep.*

What was Blake referring to in this verse? His fourfold vision is understood to refer to Eden, that place of paradise in which good and evil do not exist and where souls live in harmony. Yet how does this paradise of Eden give us a vision that is fourfold and different from the threefold vision of Beulah?[1]

For many literary critics Blake's spiritual life and writings have been read as a mystery and have been sometimes described as 'incomprehensible'.[2] This disinclination of some contemporary literary criticism to come to terms with the spiritual in Blake's poetry, or for that matter, in literature generally, should not deter the foolhardy trekker from exploring it in Blake, for whom it meant so much.

In this verse Blake's emphasis is on vision – ways of seeing – which are generated by different experiences. The paradise of a fourfold vision was, apparently, a common everyday experience for him. We learn this from reading his poetry and also from his wife who wrote to Thomas Butt complaining, 'Mr. Blake spends too much time in heaven.' Mrs. Blake's grievance had me imagining a homely scene in the Sussex cottage where Will is sitting at the kitchen table writing poetry while his wife is sweeping the floor around him. He puts out his hand to show her a grain of sand and says:

> *To see a world in a grain of sand*
> *And a heaven in a wild flower,*
> *Hold infinity in the palm of your hand*
> *And eternity in an hour.*

I imagine Mrs. Blake responding with, 'That's nice dear; now lift your feet so I can get at the sand with my broom'. But perhaps this is too harsh a view of the Blake's domestic life.

These particular lines of Blake's tell us something about ways of seeing that transcend the visible while not confusing us with ideas about place. The 'visible' in these lines are: the sand, the wild flower, your hand and the clock's face. The invisible, as understood through these lines, is eternity, infinity, heaven and the context of a world beyond the visible.

A fourfold vision represents a spiritual seeing of the world and therefore directly challenges the vulgar materialist view. The spiritual and the materialist views are explicitly contrasted here because the implications of each constitute the present undeclared Great War between spirituality and materialism. Many of us read the world about us, and that includes the texts of poetry, from a materialist and secular viewpoint. Such positions represent the orthodox view in secular culture and this means that our understanding of the world will continue to be fragmented while ever we ignore or delete the domain of Meaning.

Blake's fourfold vision was written before the fragmenting practices of materialist science had become too deeply entrenched in Western culture. His vision represents a spiritual and psychological integration, yet this is a unity any self-respecting biologist or psychologist today would not want to pursue. The safer ground for psychology is commonly seen to be located in the narrow and fragmented view provided by a focus on behaviour; formally, one that involves the statistics of rats running through mazes. As for biology and medical science, the split between mind and body is demonstrated by the manner in which medical science can dismiss mental states as placebo effects.

To fully appreciate Blake's integrated spirituality we have to stand, not on a divided ground provided by scientific materialism, but on the inclusive ground of Meaning, the territory of this short spiritual interpretative trek.

A fourfold vision is multi-layered and open to everyone, even the non-religious. This layering of meaning suggests a seeing that is profound; having a depth of meaning that has a structure similar to metaphor. This kind of integrated seeing develops through practice and usually a person needs to be 'ripened' by the repetitions of prayer or meditation before they can experience some of the basic interconnectedness of the universe. While a spiritually ripened person has the capacity to register the similarities and connections of the world, this kind of gaze goes well beyond the strictly visible and mechanical view that separates and divides.

A fourfold vision contains the knowledge that when the eye looks upon something it is actually the spirit of Meaning that is seeing; when we speak it is Meaning that is transmitted; when the ear hears the vibrations in the air it is meaning that is transmitted; when we think, it is the intelligent energy of Meaning that is being exchanged; when we love it is the unity of Meaning who loves.³ The individual who finds and knows the Spirit of Meaning finds and knows his or her true self. Like Blake's fourfold vision, such a person has all the joy of heaven.

Blake's fourfold vision represents a map of the sub-strata of our being. This layering of being is reflected by the four integrated contexts of Meaning. These four contexts of being contain both how we make meaning as well as the nature of Meaning itself, that is, both process and essence and so they represent human as well as Divine attributes and thus constitute Divine humanity. When placed alongside each other the four interrelated levels of being (Meaning) align with Blake's four-fold vision in the following manner:

Figure 1:

Fourfold Meaning:	**Blake's fourfold vision:**
4 – Symbol – abstract forms	Single vision
3 – Culture – collective habits	Twofold always
2 – Body – concrete forms	Threefold
1 – Host – essence, implicitness	Fourfold vision

Before discussing each of these levels a few general comments are necessary. The first point to note is that when aligned with the structure of being the structure of Blake's fourfold vision creates an association between ways of seeing and the various stratum levels of being. In other words, we see the world in the manner in which we make meaning. For example, if we have a tendency to make meaning that excludes, cuts up, divides and fragments then this will be the materialistic manner in which we shall see the world. In contrast, if we create meaning that is inclusive, that unifies and integrates then we will have created a fourfold spiritual vision that sees through physical forms to the underlying formlessness of Meaning. The truth-value of both these general ways of seeing rests with the inclusiveness of Meaning and not with the exclusive small materialistic picture.

The second point to note is that the four levels of Meaning appear in reverse order to Blake's fourfold vision. This is because Heaven is conventionally seen as 'up', as it is in Blake's verse, but our foundational essence is conventionally seen as a ground state, or 'down', as in fourfold Meaning. This change of direction is of little consequence in aligning these models because Meaning is everywhere and so omni-directional.

A further point about the model of fourfold being is that it has some ancient precedents. Saint Bonaventure (1221–1274) developed a theological model that had three levels of depth. Bonaventure's model involved three levels of depth understanding of the Word. Bonaventure used the 'Word' in the same way that the Stoics used 'Logos' in that the 'Word' refers to our place in the universe and how we are intimately part of the Divine. In Bonaventure's model the first level involves the uncreated Word (God) which created the incarnate Word (humanity) and then thirdly, the expressed or inspired Word (of the Bible).

What we now know about any expressions is that, whatever the medium or form, all human expressions have both a symbolic as well as a cultural context. This distinction therefore gives us four levels not three. A similar four-part depth of being is found in the work of Origen, one of the great Christian theologians of the Third Century Alexandrian School of philosophy. Origen's approach was concerned with the correct spiritual interpretation of the scriptures rather than the nature of being or Meaning. Origen suggested that when we read the scriptures there are four levels that should be remembered and taken into account in order to arrive at the full spiritual understanding of the text. Origen's four levels were: the literal, the moral, the allegorical and the Logos.[4]

Mind

Before discussing the conditions of each of the four contexts of Meaning we need to look first at a more general distinction between how we make meaning and Meaning itself. This is a distinction between the relative processes of meaning-making and the absolute essentials of the meaning of Meaning. This is an ancient distinction that has sometimes been framed as the distinction between the human and the Divine. However, a contemporary approach is to speak about Meaning. For example, the meaning we make is always contingent and relative and will involve a combination of bodily behaviours, cultural habits and symbolic expressions. As can be seen from Figure 1, these are the second, third and fourth contexts of our being, and they reflect the single, twofold and threefold visions of Blake's verse.

Linking these lines of Blake's verse with the second, third and fourth contexts of being establishes what Tibetan Buddhists understand as the ordinary mind. For Tibetan Buddhists the mind has two aspects: i) the ordinary mind of *sem,* and ii) the nature of mind or *Rigpa.*[5] The ordinary mind of *sem* is the 'discursive, dualistic, thinking mind'. In terms of Meaning, this is the mind that makes meaning through the use of symbols, cultural habits and bodily activities, and which involves the processes of Blake's threefold, twofold and single vision.

For Tibetan Buddhists, *Rigpa* is the foundation state of the ordinary mind and cannot in any way be separated from the ordinary mind. In the words of one Rinpoche the foundation of Rigpa is 'primordial, pure, pristine awareness that is at once intelligent, cognizant, radiant, and always awake. It could be said to be the knowledge of knowledge itself.'[6] This last reference to the 'knowledge of knowledge' by Sogyal Rinpoche resonates with the phrase I have been using: the *meaning of Meaning*.

Yet we could add here that the nature of mind, (the meaning of Meaning) can also be spoken of as the sight within seeing, or the light of insight, realization and awareness. This foundational divine being with its 'pristine awareness' constitutes the energy source or 'battery' that fires up the whole system of the ordinary mind and which could not possibly operate or exist on its own as a self-organizing or self-actualizing unit. The mind of humans is thus composed of both *sem* and *Rigpa* involving four layered contexts. The four-layered contexts provide a meaningful structure for what Swedenborg and Blake have both called our 'Divine Humanity'. If we are ever lucky enough to see the world through these four contexts we will experience the epiphany of a fourfold vision.

For Blake, the estate of a fourfold vision is heaven. For Tibetan Buddhists this cosmic context of awareness is 'Rigpa'; for Christians and Jews it is 'God'; for Muslims, 'al Lah'; for the ancient Stoics it was 'Logos'; and for Hindus, 'the Self'. While the terms may be different they all point to the same perennial (foundational) and Divine state. This is a universal state and like the Rigpa of Tibetan Buddhism this foundation awareness is not just host to human minds but it is the Host context to all things, physical and mental.

As another name for the creative potential of this context I have introduced the term, 'Host'. I use this term in order to move outside traditional religious sight-lines. 'Host' is also a term that implies nurturing or hosting by the forces of Nature. But what do we mean here by 'Nature'? Nature is a term commonly used to mean more than the 'environment' or the 'physical world' and even more than the romance of 'landscape'. Nature represents a combination of the Host potentials – that have a structure or 'grammar' – and the physical world, which arises for us through the perceptual and conceptual processes of the body. This combination of the Host's grammar and our bodily processes of meaning making give Nature its special spiritual sense.

We speak of Nature with a capital 'N' when the cosmic grammar of the Host is seen to be immanent within the physical world. In this sense of seeing through the physical forms, Nature becomes a feature of the fourfold vision. Nature represents a bridge between the every-day activities of the ordinary mind and the Host's support given by the underlying cosmic consciousness. This combination that exists within Nature, of the ordinary and extraordinary, of *sem* and *Rigpa*, of meaning and Meaning – represents the harmony of Nature. Hence, when we speak of the harmony of Nature we are referring to an accord between our small ordinary mind and our cosmic consciousness.

When we experience this fit, alignment or resonance it directly illuminates as the beauty of Nature. Such experiences are uplifting and essentially spiritual as they convey the realization that we are being hosted, nurtured and loved by a larger natural order. In terms of Meaning, the harmony of Nature occurs when the meaning we make fits or squares with the grammar of Meaning *per se*. In contrast, when we experience a sense of disharmony or dissociation it indicates that our ordinary mind is out of sync with the Host's conditions and laws; that is, the meaning we are making is out of balance with the laws of Meaning.

Blake's verse
What does Blake's verse of a fourfold vision add to our understanding of mind? The answer is that his verse integrates the ordinary mind into its spiritual, (cosmic) foundations. When this happens the mind recognizes itself to be part of what is perceived. When we understand Blake's fourfold vision as a joyful view of self-perceiving, then in terms of four-fold Meaning his threefold vision represents the ordinary mind's direct perception of physical objects without this realization. This is an earthly vision, which is confined to the physical world and often it strives for an exclusive focus on physical things.

A seeing which confines itself to the earthly, visible world tends also to justify that view by recourse to a philosophy of rationalist materialism. Scientific materialism looks at the sky as through a pipe and then justifies this pipe-view by saying this is necessary for the scientific method so that variables can be controlled.[7] Mechanical science has superficial similarities to Blake's rendering of a threefold vision, yet there are also important differences. Blake wrote of a threefold vision like this:

And three fold in soft Beulah's night

Blake's threefold vision corresponds to our perception of the physical world and such visual processes are set within the context of a three dimensional perceptual space. However, the three dimensional space of perception is not normally considered to be a feature of a rational, material worldview. Rather, a materialist view of space conceives of it as independent of observation and as an objective physical fact. As such, this kind of materialism locates three-dimensional space as a vacant physical reality, independent of any person's observation and through which visible objects move. In terms of Meaning, however, Blake's threefold vision refers not to an empty, objective physical space but to the implicit fullness of our perceptual processes. From this position of Meaning, Blake's threefold vision is a seeing (by our five senses) through which, and by which, the physical world comes into existence. The physical world exists therefore as appearances within our perceptual processes and not as an independent fact.

The idea, however, that the physical world is one of mere appearances is highly controversial within the orthodoxies of classical mechanics. Mechanical science is based upon the assumption that the physical world exists – as a place – independent from any observation. This is the faith of materialism, which excludes any reference to mind or Meaning and thereby finds it easy to assume the independence of the physical world.

In our contemporary culture this is also the hard-edged world of rational economics, bottom-line finance and sceptical intellectualism. Yet the weakness of materialism (and thus orthodox science) is that it does not deal with things it does not like. It has a pipe view of the sky. For example, materialists do not like to deal with meaning, language, culture, spirit, or consciousness so they simply delete, deny or ignore these factors in any scientific consideration. Hence, Blake's fourfold vision of a heavenly paradise is easily dismissed as so much religious sentimentalism.

Blake rendered a threefold vision as *soft Beulah's night*. This is a poetic image for sleep. Sleep is an apt description of materialism because the failure to realise its own incompleteness is a form of unconsciousness or sleep. At times the sleep of materialism can be celebrated and then it may become a pit of competitive and vengeful emotions that are reinforced by such credos as, 'survival of the fittest' or 'greed is good'. While materialists have faith in a dead, threefold physical world, the current and more moderate view of Meaning holds that a threefold vision is entirely essential in order to produce a fourfold multi-layered spiritual vision of grace and beauty. This is the vision of Nature that commands our attention because its aesthetic authority and wholeness exists beyond the explicit details of the physical landscape.

Yet if, like materialists, we should blind ourselves to the spiritual then in relation to the physical world we will be left not with the beauty of Nature but with the stale idea of a separate, dead and independent physical place where objects move through a four dimensional continuum. Note that here I have referred to a four-dimensional continuum rather than the three dimensions of space. The fourth dimension represents that of time.

Yet is time part of the physical world? For the materialist, time is a physical fact divorced from any consideration of Meaning. This view of time is similar to you speaking and telling me you have no tongue. To conceive of time while dismissing the mind that has done the conceiving is one of the central contradictions of materialism. Yet for those many scientists who hold to such contradictions, time is a physical condition that would allow us to travel through it, see for example, Paul Davies (2002) *How to Build a Time Machine*, London: Penguin. The conclusion of time travel follows logically once Meaning and the processes of seeing have been deleted from consideration. With this pair of limiting spectacles we are easily able to transform the concept of time into something that is objective and concrete. Physical time is thus a feature of looking at the sky through a pipe. In contrast, when we include Meaning in our considerations of time this dimension is immediately seen not as physical event but as one of the features of Blake's fourfold vision.

To understand how time is part of the fourfold vision we need to return to Blake's verse. After the threefold vision of *soft Beulah's night* he wrote:

And twofold Always.

What does it mean for a vision to be 'twofold always'? Some purchase on this question comes from the essay, *Compensations* by Ralph Waldo Emerson[8] who wrote on polarity:

POLARITY, or action and reaction, we meet in every part of nature; in darkness and light; in heat and cold; in the ebb and flow of waters; in male and female; in the inspiration and expiration of plants and animals; in the equation of quantity and quality in the fluids of the animal body; in the systole and diastole of the heart; in the undulations of fluids, and of sound; in the centrifugal and centripetal gravity; in electricity, galvanism, and chemical affinity .... An inevitable dualism bisects nature, so that each thing is a half, and suggests another thing to make it whole; as, spirit, matter; man, woman; odd, even; subjective, objective; in, out; upper, under; motion, rest; yea, nay. Whilst the world is thus dual, so is every one of its parts.

Emerson here agrees with Blake – if 'the world is thus dual' then it is 'twofold always'. This is not the end of the matter, however, because while the world is 'twofold always' this dualism, as some materialists would argue, is reduced to the subjective ability to categorise, name and classify. In addition, materialists would say that the objective world is independent and separate from the subjective way we think. If this materialistic statement were true then we could say nothing objective about the world because everything we say necessarily involves the dualism of categorizing, naming and classifying. The impossibility of moving beyond the dualism of the meaning we make thus provides us with a world that is twofold always. And this is so and not otherwise because we humans are participants in Nature and not objective observers.

Like Blake's threefold vision the dualism of 'twofold always' can open us to the splendors of a fourfold vision of grace and heaven. Alternatively, we can use dualism to reduce our vision and ourselves by closing off the splendour of a spiritual life. Such closures happen when the normal dualism of meaning (Meaning and meaning or the codes of implicit and explicit) is over-emphasised so it becomes a binary oppositional statement. In a social situation, such oppositional conditions take on the clothes of a moral code expressed in terms of *us versus them*. This two-valued exclusive either/or code represents the underlying moral stance of all tribes, ancient and modern, ethnic, religious or secular. Hence the conundrum which each of us is faced with in Blake's 'twofold always' is how the world of dualisms can be part of a larger fourfold vision.

Blake's verse already gives us a clue how to solve this problem. Inherent in the multi-layered structure of his fourfold vision are the holistic links that integrate us with our vision. Emerson also points us in this direction through his use of the argument that a certain compensation exists within every dualism. Emerson says that 'a certain compensation balances every gift and every defect'. For Emerson, one part of every dualism is always compensated by the other part in such a manner that there is a balance operating between the two parts of a polarity. We only have to think of the compensation that balances the male and female of every species. With the idea of balance come connection and integration within a larger contextual framework, such as a fourfold vision.

The dualism of 'twofold always' therefore does not have to become a set of closed binary differences that separate and divide, but rather they exist as a series of distinctions that connect within larger, open holistic patterns. The essential first step towards recognising divinity in all is the acceptance of contrary states of being. This is an ancient message. It is a message that comes to us from the 'middle path' of Buddhism. Another example is the Hindu deity of Shiva in the form of Ardhanari, which expresses this kind of balancing compensation. Ardhanari is the beautiful standing figure of half man/half woman that speaks to us of the compensation that exists between male and female forms. This figure, which is a deity, conveys to us a necessary balance of forces that exists within a larger fourfold vision of paradise. In other cultures there are similar models operating; for example, in Chinese medicine there is the dynamic balance of forces expressed in the notions of yin and yang.

Given Blake's 'twofold always' and Emerson's 'the world is thus dual' how can we understand the nature of time? Time is normally represented as an 'arrow' with three states: past, present and future. How can these three elements of time be dual? When he began his essay on *Compensations* Emerson expressed the view that time was dual with the line:

The wings of Time are black and white,

The orthodox scientific view of time as an arrow challenges the idea of it having dual states. What then could possibly constitute time's dualism? The answer to this question is that the wings of time always move backwards and forwards: to the past and to the future. The wings of time are created by our explicit measurements that point backwards or forwards. It is the flapping of these wings (our measurements) that create time. But what of the 'flapper', the energy source that causes the wings to flap? I refer here to the fulcrum or balance point between the two wings, which we usually nominate as 'the present moment' or 'NOW'. The present moment has no measurements because it cannot be measured. Rather, it represents the potentials for making measurements. 'NOW' is an essence, an energy potential which can also be referred to as a non-personal '*I am-ness*'. The fulcrum or centre that is '*I am*' happens to be non-personal because the present moment is generic to everyone.

This generic energy potential of the present moment NOW reflects what God is reported to have said to Moses: '*I am that I am*'. Thus the *I am* of the present is also God's implicit energy force (Spirit) operating through us. This undifferentiated potential is transformed through our conceptual abilities when they are involved in the abstract measurements of movements, and the results constitute the wings of time: the movements of past and future. Without this cosmic potential of NOW, without this God given *I am-ness,* there would be no measurement of anything and hence no time. Time's dualism, the past and future wings of time, therefore rests on the balance potentials of NOW, what we call the present moment. All spiritual aspirants who seek to fully realize their true natures through contemplation, prayer or mediation attempt to focus on the undifferentiated state of NOW.

While the past and the future are measurable, the NOW of the present is unmeasurable. By 'unmeasurable' I mean not able to be measured: non-computational. We are unable to measure the present because it is constituted by the potentials of implicitness (implicit meaning) whereas all measurements are constituted through expressions that contain explicit and differential meaning. As explicit meaning is absolutely necessary for any measurement to occur, a state of complete implicitness cannot be measured. Such implicitness represents the potentials of NOW.

The dual wings of time are also constituted through conceptual processes; processes we commonly call thoughts. Albert Einstein agreed with this when he was reported to have said in 1941, some thirty years after he developed his theories of relativity, 'time and space are modes by which we think and not conditions in which we live'.[9] Implicit in Einstein's words is the scientific view that the conditions in which we live are objective and physical and our modes of thinking are personal and subjective. Einstein's materialist view is, of course, not part of the fourfold vision expressed here. Nevertheless, we find common ground with his claim that time (the wings of time) are modes of thought: they are conceptual.

Because the wings of time are created by concepts they cannot be part of the three dimensions of space that are immediately perceivable – visible. In other words, the wings of time are invisible, as are all concepts. We may see a concept in our 'mind's eye' but we do not see a concept with our eyes. We therefore do not perceive time; rather we are only able to conceive of time. This distinction between the visible of space and the invisible of concepts that create time indicates that the orthodox metaphor of the 'arrow of time' that travels through a four-dimensional space/time continuum is false and confusing.[10] From Blake's perspective of a fourfold vision, a four-dimensional space/time continuum is not a separate, objective and independent event but rather an event within the mind. Such a continuum of mind involves the three dimensions of sense perception as well as the one dimension of concept formation. This event of mind operates within and between the four levels as rendered by Blake's verse, that is, encompassing a threefold, a twofold and a single vision.

The final lines in Blake's verse provide us with a prayer:

May God us keep
From single vision & Newton's sleep.

These lines refer to the possible negative effects of using language and symbols in an autocratic and single manner. A single vision is created through the use of language and signs when they produce single meanings. This limited and often linear kind of vision comes from literal and surface readings or renderings of any text, whether scientific or religious. A single vision also comes from the single value we place on finance or technology.

These lines from Blake's verse imply that Newton's mechanical science creates the sleep of a literal vision. Mechanical and orthodox technology and science rest on axiomatic and factual knowledge that eschews uncertainty and ambiguity to such a degree that this kind of knowledge commonly manufactures the sleep of a single vision. Yet the sleep of single vision is broader than mechanical science and technology for it is also a common method of seeing in our contemporary culture. It is the vision of the tabloid media as well as the one we lapse into when we are over-stressed or in crisis. It is also the vision of the religious fundamentalist who is willing to fight and sometimes die to keep the ignorance of his single vision strong.

The sleep of single vision is also common to the corporation (which is a symbolic entity) whose bottom line is represented by the symbols of finance. The exchange value of money creates in us a single vision. The exchange value of the symbols we call money also create the driving force within most corporations. When the fourfold life of society is valued only for the exchange value of goods and services, we then create the single meaning of price. When this happens we become the one-dimensional consumer that has an exclusive focus on price, which automatically provides us with a single vision of the world with its consequent morality: 'everyone has a price'. For those who pursue or celebrate the sleep of a single vision or the hapless life of binary opposites then Blake's heaven, which is created by a fourfold vision, can never be realized.

Blake's fourfold vision sets before us the optimistic promise of seeing life in context, that is, of seeing the big picture. In this sense, 'in context' refers to a seeing that takes into account the four contexts of mind that Blake refers to in his verse. These four contexts also represent four integrated levels of Meaning and therefore four contexts of being.

In summary, climbing Blake's Pass is a difficult exercise if one is suffering from the amnesia of a single vision or the antagonism of binary opposites. These kinds of sleep prevent us from ripening spiritually and hence from seeing the summits of the big picture. These unfortunate conditions commonly lead those who see life in surface forms to exaggerate, celebrate or even proselytize their illusionary benefits. Yet the consequences of looking at the sky through a pipe are multiple and can be grouped under the heading of *the deletion or ignorance of contextual meaning*. We can see this deletion in the literal views of mechanical science and technology where the contexts of mind, culture, symbols and Meaning are always deleted. In the tabloid media, for example, what normally is erased are the contexts of culture and the environment as well as the financial interests of the publisher, while corporations tend to omit the wider context of the planet's environment from their balance sheets.

Chapter 4 – Communal Base Camp

Psychology is supposed to be the science of mental life. This was the title to a psychology textbook written in the 1960s by George A. Miller. As Miller says in his first chapter, mental life seemed to be a well defined thing in the 1890s, but by he time he wrote his book some seventy years later 'we are less certain'.[1] He goes on to say that the modern mind seems to be concealed from view. I write some fifty years after Miller and the situation has changed little. Psychologists and philosophers are still unable to adequately define mental life today.

The cause of this lack of clarity could fill a PhD dissertation, suffice to say that my experience as a psychological counsellor has led me to believe that while psychology in general can explain a good deal about human behavior it is seriously deficient when it comes to defining mental life and mental health in particular. The short answer for why this is so is that psychology has its roots in the materialism of biology and cannot escape that limitation. The materialist view represents mental life as a by-product of brain activity and this is a wretched way to approach the problem of defining mental life. Yet that branch of analytic philosophy called the philosophy of mind has done little better. There is a whole battalion of analytical philosophers who are noted mostly for the abstractness of their terminology and diversity of their approaches. The net result has been a fragmentation of approaches that has taken us no closer to having mental life illuminated.

The approach taken here is not built upon the excluding

traditions of psychology or the cerebral views of analytical philosophers. Rather, this analysis of mental life develops out of a holistic discussion of Meaning. Like an inclusive democracy, Meaning has a variety of different aspects that together make up a whole. Mental life represents these aspects and as a consequence of this integration we can say that the content of all mental life is meaning. This means that the relationships of Meaning constitute the very processes of knowing, of cognition and, as well, these relationships construct the being, that is, the nature of the knower. We can, therefore, discuss mind and intelligence in terms of the relationships of Meaning, for every exchange of Meaning (and meaning) will always convey and involve some awareness and intelligence.[2] Awareness and intelligence are therefore not separate from the relationships of Meaning or from meaning exchanges.

The conventional psychological and philosophical view of mind assumes that awareness and meaning are separate as well as assuming that each mind is separate from every other and from the environment. The idea of separate minds is a feature of the belief that we are separate, autonomous individuals. In other words, each person is assumed to have his or her own private mind, or what can be called a solo mind, which is self-organizing or creates its own self-organization. In terms of Meaning, these assumptions about separate minds arise from a failure to appreciate and give value to the interconnected nature of Meaning. There can be no autonomous solo minds that belong to separate individuals because there are no splits or separations in this universe where everything is fundamentally interconnected.

As discussed earlier, the first law of Meaning stipulates that we live in a universe that is absolutely interconnected. This is our universe where Meaning is everywhere present. From the most distant star to the smallest particle, Meaning is discovered through the structure of its connections, links and relationships.

A focus on Meaning amounts to a focus on relationships. The logic of an interconnected universe implies there are no separate, autonomous individual things or identities simply because every feature, element, state, and mind, is inseparably interconnected to its neighbor and to the cosmos. As Meaning is absolutely interconnected it follows that the minds of all people are also absolutely interconnected.

As a consequence of the absolute interconnections of Meaning there cannot be separate or solo minds. The ordinary mind of an individual is therefore not a self-organizing, separate or private entity. Within the perspective of Meaning, the ordinary mind of an individual has an individual structure that rests on, and is supported by, the integrated singular and cosmic consciousness of the universe – the meaning of Meaning: the Host (God). Each individual will therefore directly and collectively participate in a holographic interconnection with the One cosmic consciousness of the Host context. Such participation is discovered whenever we come in contact with its unifying presence, which flows just below the surface of the everyday ordinary mind.

The ordinary mind (*sem* for Tibetan Buddhists) can be liken to the turbulence of local weather patterns that exist as distinct features of larger climatic patterns. The turbulence, which produces the ordinary mind, comes from the meanings we create that swirl around the second, third and fourth levels of the fourfold self. In other words, these circular eddies of meanings are set up by the contexts of bodily activity, by collective habitual actions, and by our use of signs and symbols. A model of the ordinary mind is as follows:

The ordinary mind:
4 – Symbol – abstract forms
3 – Culture – collective habits
2 – Body – concrete forms

From the point of view of Meaning, our ordinary minds are not private but communal and cosmic and hence entirely non-private. Of the three contexts of the ordinary mind, only the body context could suggest a personal or private mental domain. The other two contexts of mind (symbols and culture) are usually seen as social and collective in their nature and therefore entirely non-personal.

It may be argued that the body context suggests the idea of a private person because each of us has a unique body and this body occupies a separate space from all other bodies. While these differences (of space) are to be acknowledged they do not constitute differences that separate the body from its environment or from the underlying cosmic influences of Meaning. Rather, all the meanings created by the body context are part of the fourfold context of our being: of Meaning. There are two more features of the mind that now need to be integrated into the turbulence of these three contexts of mind. These are the features of implicit and explicit mind.

Implicit and explicit mind

The ordinary mind includes the meaning of differences and distinctions and these are made up by the distinctions found in our use of language as well the differences that arise from cultural interactions and also from the differences created by the body's activities. Differences and distinctions *per se* constitute the conscious and visible aspect of the ordinary mind. These explicit features therefore constitute the visible content of the conscious mind and hence we can say that differences and distinctions create the conscious mind's visible contents. In other words, there is no visible content of the conscious mind other than that which is explicit, distinct and differential. From the big-picture perspective, explicit meaning makes up perhaps as little as five to ten percentiles of our entire mind.

The other composite feature of mind is implicit meaning,

which perhaps makes up the rest; ninety percentiles. Our implicit mind represents the big-picture mind and by this I mean that our implicit mind is composed of the implicit connections, links and relationships embedded within the four contexts of being. Within the ordinary mind, however, implicit meaning should not be confused with what in common psychological language is called the unconscious mind, or what in Freudian psychoanalysis is called the repressed. Even though the implicit mind is highly influential and somewhat hidden it is far broader and deeper than Freud's ideas about the unconscious and repression.[3]

As the greater part of the ordinary mind is built upon a contextual and implicit structure it means that the entire range of mental states and syndromes of the ordinary conscious mind (involving emotions, perceptions, conceptions, cognitions, habits, intuitions and so on) are composed of a gestalt in which a small, focused foreground of explicit differences interact with each other within a large contextual canvass of implicit meaning. The distinctions and differences that make up the visible part of the conscious mind arise quite naturally through our perception and use of symbols (in particular, language), through our use of cultural artifacts and habits and norms of thinking, and finally, through the meanings we construct through behavior and emotions.

Note I have been using the pronoun 'our' to describe the meanings we make in the constructions of our conscious minds. Yet I have also said that the ordinary mind is non-personal. How do these positions fit together? In other words, how is it possible to have the idea of 'a conscious subjectivity' that is not a personal or private state? This question is often put in the oppositional language of freedom of choice versus determinism. Such language has nothing to say about Meaning and with its emphasis on oppositional states it tends to pre-empt the question of how it is possible for a person to have a non-personal ordinary mind.

Agency

If I slant this question towards the idea of causality we can get a better purchase on it. Instead of speaking about the personal and non-personal we can speak about agency. Agency is a causal idea and it is the thread that runs through and within the question of freedom of choice versus determinism. If we now ask: does the ordinary mind have agency, and if so how does it operate, the answer readily comes from the model of fourfold Meaning. This model tells us that the agency of the mind has four parts. In other words, it is a four-part agency. As there are three parts to the ordinary mind of an individual so there are three kinds of agency within that ordinary mind. These are: the agency of symbols, the agency of culture and the agency of the body.

The body's secondary location (as the second context of mind) means that it does not have its own nature, or put another way, the body is not self-caused or fully autonomous. It does not cause its own birth nor can it prevent its own death. The causality which belongs to the body is always conditional and constrained by the manner in which it operates and also by the cosmic influences of Meaning that created it in the first place and which organize it during its growth and maturation and that will finally enfold it back into the cosmos from whence it came. The body's organization and agency is therefore always relative and derivative. Similar observations can be made about our use of symbols and culture. I discuss this in the next chapter.

While these three agencies of symbols, culture and the body are different one from another, they nevertheless share a common condition. Each has an agency that is derivative and conditional and, therefore, relative. This means that the organizational and causal authority of each context of the ordinary mind is conditional upon the first fundamental context of Meaning, which is the Host context. Taken together the three derivative agencies of the ordinary mind do not add up to a separate self-organizing unit that has autonomy. In other words, these three derivative agencies acting together cannot create a solo mind that has a separate identity. This conditional situation exists even when one thousand people speak together as one voice. For example, even an overwhelming vote in favor of a question like infallibility can never add up to, or create, an infallible, absolute autonomous agency.

Only the meaning of Meaning, the Host context, is absolute in terms of autonomy and causality and infallible in terms of truth. One way to bring out the distinction between the relative agency of the ordinary mind and the absolute agency of the Host context is the question of morality. If we should look for the foundations of our moral code in the psychology of autonomous agents, for instance in our attitudes towards happiness, suffering or justice then we will have created a relative and conditional moral system yet we will be inclined to think of this system as absolute. This reversal: of the ordinary mind becoming absolute, tends to be the inclination of both secular liberals and religious conservatives who assume that the idea of autonomous agents provide us with a solid foundation for morality and who also understand virtue to be socially constructed and socially learned. Such socially constructed virtues are naturally norm-based and, as such, conditional upon the relative social norms that spawn them.

A moral code that does not suffer from the relativities of norm-based conditions and is not based upon the fiction of autonomous agents is one that has its foundations in the laws of Meaning. As these laws are unconditional and absolute, a moral code that mirrors these laws will tend to establish absolute and unconditional standards. What could those standards look like? There are several well-known moral values that come to us from history and which reflect the laws of Meaning. For example, *unity within diversity* is the social goal of inclusive secular democracies as well as being the principle at work in all healthy ecological systems. It represents the moral stance of a civilized, open-minded society that deals with social, religious, gender and ethnic differences not by suppressing them or over-valuing a particular kind so it becomes a cause that divides, but by accepting such differences as the necessary tapestry of a healthy community. *Unity within diversity* represents a moral principle, which reflects the laws of Meaning and hence is unconditional in terms of a particular society, culture or epoch.

Returning to the vertical structure of the individual's mind, it is comprised of three parts that have relative and conditional authority – we can use the term 'relative autonomy' here – and one part that has absolute autonomy. This mixture of the relative with the absolute sets the stage for the drama of human existence. This drama is usually a tragedy in which the relative and ordinary mind may feel the need for perfection but does not possess the knowledge needed to achieve this harmonious state. The script of this tragedy follows a well-worn path: an individual seeks perfection, not within the implicitness of the Host context but within his/her ordinary mind, that is, through the use of language, or through social approval, or through body shape or sporting or artistic achievement. Such relative and conditional pathways are doomed to frustration and failure. The story of this human tragedy is supported and reinforced by the belief in a private self in control of its destiny. This false belief, broadly called 'individualism', is a widespread pathology. It rests on the assumption that each of us has a private and separate mind which has available to it the freedom of choice that comes with self-autonomy.

This sense of personal autonomy and unrestricted freedom of choice arises not from a clearly defined understanding of the mind but from the confusion that comes from welding together the four agencies of mind into a single perfect identity that is believed to have causality, ownership and a property called 'mine'. Yet there is actually nothing personal about the structure of the ordinary mind. The relative autonomy that is a feature of the ordinary mind arises not from some idiosyncratic personal and unique self but from the creative turbulence of the meanings we make. The meaning we make is always secondary to Meaning, which is the source and battery that powers up the whole complex system of the ordinary mind. Specifically, the relative autonomy of the ordinary mind comes from the provisional agency of the way symbols interact, together with the conditional nature of cultural beliefs and habits, and also from the physical yet derivative nature of the body's organization. In addition, there is also nothing personal about the first level of mind: the perfect meaning of Meaning – the Host context. This is the realm of cosmic consciousness, which in essence is universal.

Human nature
In terms of Meaning, those who act selfishly and without regard for their neighbors are at war with the communal nature of their own minds and so will tend to act in an antisocial or asocial manner. The integrated nature of the four levels of mind suggests that in order to create harmony and so act in conforming with this communal reality of our minds we should have a degree of self-knowledge. In other words we must first become acquainted with the communal nature of our minds and the laws of Meaning. Specifically, this means becoming acquainted with the relative agency of the symbols we use, the persuasions of the culture we live in and of our body's special organization, but in addition, it is overwhelmingly important to have some appreciation and experience of the unifying agency of the Host context. This kind of self-knowledge is the most important knowledge humans can have. This self-reflective knowledge makes us human as well as defining us as distinct from all other organisms.

Human nature – the nature of the human mind – is thus essentially collective, highly interconnected and holographic. There is nothing about the mind that is private, personal or separate, except perhaps the illusion that it is so. This is the case because there is nothing about Meaning that is private, personal or separate. In other words, relationships of meaning are always social and communal. Relationships are never private in the sense that they are separate or divorced from the universe-wide community of relationships. This communal view of human nature is based upon the interconnected nature of Meaning and the relational structure of meaning. This view of Meaning challenges materialism, which is inclined to say that brains create the private and local worlds of personal and private subjectivity. It also challenges the pessimistic idea of an isolated soul lost in a world he never made. The English philosopher Thomas Hobbes (1566–1679) made famous the pessimistic belief in our natural alienation by his statement that man's life was 'solitary, poor, nasty, brutish and short'.

The great thinkers of ancient Greece and Rome did not, however, share Hobbes' pessimism. Plato and Aristotle held that human nature inclined towards the good and the true, which is a position that reflects the interconnected relational nature of Meaning. Aristotle even believed that we are first and foremost, 'political creatures' who delight in the mutual recognition of universal law, justice and the common good.[4] I would suggest that the reason why we are political creatures in the broad sense is that our minds are essentially communal and therefore participatory and such participation makes us political.

Those of us who selflessly participate in social and communal activities do so by conforming to the communal nature of our ordinary minds and such activity thereby creates reciprocal relationships that exchange social harmony through acts of kindness. Because minds are inherently communal we are inherently our brother's keeper because our brother, sister, father and mother represent those sets of communal relationships which have helped construct the complex set of spiral relationships that is our ordinary mind. On this point, it is interesting to note that Jesus is reported to have said (Mark 3: 13), 'Whoever does God's will is my brother and sister and mother'. Such a moral statement is in keeping with the idea that the ordinary mind should try and work in harmony with the cosmic mind of God: the Host context.

In terms of Meaning, 'God's will' represents the laws, codes and states of Meaning. The first law of Meaning says that we live in a universe where everything is interconnected and hence communal. What is more, creating social harmony by conforming to the laws of Meaning (to God's will) is a general human response not confined to any particular religion, ethnic group, skin color or region. Another moral principle based upon the laws of Meaning is the statement that we should love 'thy neighbor as thyself' (Luke, 10: 27), because the act of doing so helps us realize the communal nature of who we are. Such actions, which carry the potential for self-realization, are available to everyone no matter who they are. And for those who do act in this communal interconnected manner the boon is the realization that we are part of one another; or in other words, we are the turbulence caused by exchange relationships within the climate of One cosmic consciousness.

For many, however, the idea that there is nothing private, personal or separate about their minds is a horrifying concept. The awful sense that we are simply interconnected communal relationships may appear too difficult an idea for many who perhaps live by an entrepreneurial credo; or who have a strong desire to make a name for themselves; or who simply do not want to pay their taxes. In other words, the rejection of the communal and participatory, interconnected nature of our minds will tend to force many of us into the illusion of a private, entrepreneurial prison-house called 'mine'. In order to challenge the idea that we are nothing but a particular swirl of communal relationships, the determined entrepreneur may argue that I have been writing about the meaning of *I am* and surely this phrase indicates a private center of intention or willfulness that is beyond the provisional status of communal relationships?

In reply I would say that my intentions do not mark out a private self but instead represent the influences of several features such as education, the knowledge I have accumulated and an attitude towards learning. Each of these is an aspect of Meaning. I might also say that the center of my intentions – 'me' – is actually a dynamic landscape of Meaning. In addition, within this dynamic landscape there are also the potentials to make meaning. Some of these potentials relate to the idea of destiny. One's destiny represents the particular pathway that has been laid out for each of us to tread in this lifetime. Learning to value, know and understand one's destiny involves the practice of listening to the subtle messages that come on the wind and through the heart.

This is an intuitive learning that is not taught in institutions of higher learning, but comes from the Meaning within. I did not manufacture the destiny of this self; rather it has come as a gift from the potentials of Meaning so that this particular mind called Andrew may evolve through learning. As a consequence, neither intention nor destiny has created a separate private self and that means freedom of choice is always limited to a set of relative and conditional actions. These actions arise from a choice we can make either to accept or resist – for instance – our destiny, or more broadly the hierarchy of the four levels of mind and the idea of a transcendent and absolute Divinity. Thus freedom of choice boils down to accepting or resisting what is given in the laws and conditions of Meaning.

Resisting the conditions and laws of Meaning creates the drama of human existence. Yet there are some potentials of the Host context that none of us resist. We do not resist them because most people pay little or no regard to these potentials that are given by the Host context. One example of such potentials relates to our intelligence and the way in which these intelligent potentials work within our ordinary minds to combine perceptions with ideas to form concepts, systems and models. Another example is the potentials of the sight within the mechanics of our seeing. Without this inner sight there is no seeing, no sense perception at all. Another example is the inner sight of the 'mind's eye' that is often called our imagination. Yet another example is the inner sight of 'insight', 'realization' and 'intuition'. Without these several inner sights there is no mind, life or energy within a body. A body without these inner sights is dead.

Furthermore, the luminosity of these inner sights that create 'seeing' is a perfect and steady energy state and it is because of this steady energy state that the ordinary mind is able to function at all. Hence this steady state of inner luminosity is not a feature of the ordinary provisional mind but a state of the meaning of Meaning – the Host context. It is a perfect state with which all spiritual aspirants aspire to merge. Our luminous sight/center (some have called it our 'heart sight') represents the essential ground of '*I am*'. As this luminous center emanates from the universal foundational context of our cosmic mind, (Rigpa, God, the meaning of Meaning) it is not personal or private in any sense.

The commonly asked question about my relationship to God is therefore actually a question about a relationship to my-self, or in other words, the question of who I am. In terms of Meaning, this question leads on to unraveling the four levels of mind.

In summary, the base camp of the ordinary mind is not a by-product of brain activity (the materialist view). Neither is it a private, autonomous mental (subjective) state that is opposed in some manner to an objective physical world. It is, rather, a complex communal and dynamic set of circular relationships, which have four vertical levels: *symbols, culture, body and Host*. The mind also has a gestalt structure with perhaps ten per cent of it being explicit while the vast majority of its relations are implicit. The three levels of the ordinary mind are conditional and relative to the first and foundational context of mind: the Host context. The differences between these two, our ordinary mind and our cosmic mind, create the drama of our human existence. Within our cosmic mind lie the potentials of our luminous sight center as well as the unfolding potentials of our destiny. In the next chapter I will look at how the ordinary mind evolves and transforms through learning.

Chapter 5 – The weather of becoming

In the early 1990s I was a member of a small group called Academics for Justice. We were made up mainly of academics from the disciplines of law, sociology and applied linguistics. We worked voluntarily on a series of miscarriages of justice cases. One of the more celebrated cases became known as the Hilton Bombing case. It arose out of an incident on the 13th February 1978 when a bomb exploded outside Sydney's Hilton Hotel where various heads of government were gathered for the Commonwealth Heads of Government Regional Meeting (CHOGRM). The blast killed two council workers and a policemen while another policemen was seriously wounded.

This case was interesting and complex as it involved four miscarriages of justice and another man who was sent to prison for confessing to a crime he did not commit. I have had a life-long interest in justice systems and the influences that lead a system to fail. In democratic states justice systems can fail for many reasons, but the overriding reason they fail is that court hearings have neglected some important truth. In terms of justice *per se* as distinct from justice systems, the concept of justice can become clouded if we identify it with concepts of fate or divine Providence or as part of the cosmic plan.

This common but incorrect identification was the view reflected in a play by Elie Wiesel called, *The Trial of God (as it was held on February 25, 1649, in Shamgorod)*. This is a play about a fictitious trial where God is called, in absentia, as the defendant. The point of the play is the theological question, which the Old Testament Book of Job raises: can people understand God to be just in light of the all-pervasive suffering in the world? In terms of Meaning, this is a wrongheaded question. Justice, or ideas of 'the just' are not part of the nature of God; rather they are associated with social consequences. Yet if we conceive of God as some kind of master magician who dispenses justice, and perhaps miracles, then the idea that this super-personality is 'just' may make some sense. However, if we do see God as a super-personality then the question that the Book of Job raises is difficult if not impossible to answer.

In contrast to the super-personality, when God is understood as the Meaning within us so we exist as part of Divine humanity then the laws of Meaning may provide us with some understanding of where justice fits in the scheme of things. For example, there is nothing in the laws of Meaning that would lead me to believe that justice was an inherent feature of them. The Book of Job seems to agree with this point for Job is a righteous person who fears God, yet God multiplies Job's miseries. The story of Job, therefore, points us away from the interpretation that justice is dispensed by God-as-a-super-personality and towards the more obvious reading that our ideas of justice are within the social realm. How then does justice relate to our ideas of God?

One way to answer this question is to look at the order of the universe, which can be observed in the transient nature of all visible objects and forms. This order of transience means that every visible object or form has a birth or beginning, followed by a period of unfolding, and then by a period of enfolding until the visible object disappears back into the implicitness from whence it came. The circular trajectory of these transformations, together with the cosmic energy that propels them speaks directly to the second and third laws of Meaning: *circularity* and *omnipotence*. In other words, the order created by the circular transience of all objects is an inherent feature of the Host context of mind.

The order of this circular transience is universal, which means it applies to the ordinary mind as well as to what we commonly understand as the physical world. When applied to the ordinary mind these transformations indicate a series of changes and developments within the ordinary mind that can be spoken about simply as learning. Hence learning is much more than a method of enhancing skills and acquiring social status. It is also the pathway of becoming and therefore unlike ideas and systems of justice, learning represents a set of innate maturation processes that mark off the various modes of the human mind.

From a big picture perspective of Meaning, if learning is an innate maturation process then every person is moving along a pre-determined learning path whether he/she wants to be on it or not. This pathway is as inevitable as the wind. Some of us may travel a great distance along the path of becoming within one lifetime, while others may develop all kinds of habits that delay and resist the subtle and continuous pressure for change. The inevitability of learning arises out of the natural and inevitable movement and transformations of meaning (discussed shortly). Thus within the ordinary mind learning is a continual process whether we are awake or asleep and it happens beyond our control.

How ideas of a just God relate to the inevitability of learning is interesting. For example, if we assume a super-personality-God that is just, then we can blame him for our sense of injustice and hurt. When we blame God for the suffering in the world our blame automatically inhibits our learning. Blame and learning are opposing attitudes; one is shut the other is open. Learning needs an open mind so that the mind can change our habits of behavior and negative tendencies; on the other hand, blame closes the mind in a manner that resists self-reflection as well as what is changing around us. The inevitability of learning means that the drive to learn is not a private motivational force and as a consequence the impetus to learn is not manufactured by the relative and conditional features of the ordinary mind.

There is, therefore, no separate individual will to learn. Rather, learning is an innate transformational movement of Meaning. Living in this contemporary society we can enhance this innate drive to learn through formal educational programs provided by schools and institutions of higher learning. However, even though our modern societies are geared to produce highly educated citizens, we humans do not have freedom of choice about deciding in the first place whether to learn or not. Our patterns of learning are closely associated with patterns of growth; of birth, development and death, and we do not have much choice about these changes.

As a result of this continual innate pressure to learn that is associated with subtle maturation and developmental changes, we are sometimes forced into situations that do not please us. When this happens we tend to resist what is happening and this leads to stress and anxiety, or worse. For example, as we grow older we will be forced into new learning situations that can cause a crisis in mid-life, or later when we leave the workforce. In extreme situations such crises can result in mental breakdowns. A mental breakdown represents the sudden collapse of our resistance to the inevitable changes that are part of the learning path of becoming. A mental breakdown represents a complete withdrawal from trying to stop the inevitable changes that come upon us. Mental breakdowns will, therefore, be characterized by a sense of giving in, or giving up, as well as a letting go of old ideas and habits of behavior, but they have healthy outcomes in that they provide the opportunity for us to learn, mature and move in harmony with the inevitable changes of this transient world.

Within the ordinary mind, meaning is transformed not randomly but in an ordered three-step process. Learning any activity and becoming proficient in it represents a three-step movement through an ordered circular arc involving a series of predictable changes and transformation. The three steps in the arc of learning are: *identification, differentiation and integration.* These three steps are involved in everything we learn, regardless of the age of the learner and the following model indicates them:

Figure 2: The arc of learning:

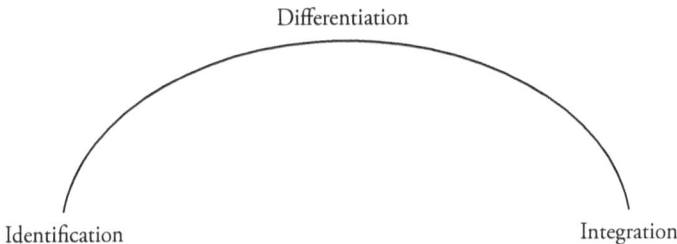

The first thing we need to recognize about this model is that it represents what happens within the ordinary mind. The ordinary mind is made up of three layers (*symbols, culture and body*) and is supported by the implicit Meaning of the cosmic Host context. If we were to show a diagram of learning that took account of the Host context it would become a circle. The bottom of the circle represents the domain in which there are the potentials of memory and these are both a source and a repository of learning.[1]

During our lifetime we learn many things; some things we learn quickly, others take a long time. All learning occurs in circles that encompass memory, which is located within the context of the Host. This is the case from the small circles of learning (how to tie your shoelace) to the larger circles (how to get on with your neighbors). Different sized circles also have different names. The smaller circles of formal education tend to be called learning programs. Larger circles that extend over some years tend to be called periods of development or maturation. Even larger circles that extend over millenniums can be called cultural stages in the evolution of consciousness.

The focus in this chapter, however, is a partial view of learning because we are focused here on learning within the ordinary mind. The model above is therefore an arc rather than a circle. An arc is a portion of a circle in the same way as the ordinary mind is a small portion of our whole mind, which by necessity includes a memory potential within the Host context. It is also important to have this partial view in order to come to some understanding of the three learning steps in the ordinary mind. These three steps are our focus here.

To be proficient in any area of endeavor we have to travel through the steps of *identification, differentiation and integration*. Progress through this arc of learning is inevitable in order to master, for example, a musical instrument, a second language, a sport and in the long term, a spiritual life. While we may choose individual learning programs during our formal education as well as a variety of activities for our informal education, we cannot choose **not** to learn anything so that, for example, our mental development and maturation stop. The movement of learning is the movement of becoming and this movement is a continual and dynamic process.

Three transformations

The underlying structure of the arc of learning comes from a series of transformations of Meaning. For example, in the first step of identification there is a change that unfolds meaning. This unfolding occurs when some aspect of implicit Meaning is transformed into some feature of explicit meaning. This is a transformation from *implicit to explicit* meaning. This change provides the structural basis for the processes of identification. Hence, identification processes involve those instances where the underlying implicitness of the Host context has generated a series of explicit distinctions that are linked together to create explicit, visible and conscious forms that we then recognize as such.

Explicit forms constitute much of the content of the conscious mind. The conscious mind represents that section of the ordinary mind that is limited to the creation and the interaction of explicit forms and meaning. The conscious mind involves the three steps of learning but is limited to the exchanges of explicit distinctions. We could say that the conscious mind is simply the visible tip of the ordinary mind. I have found it more productive to speak of explicit meaning rather than to speak of the conscious mind. This is because the term 'conscious mind', when used in its psychological sense, tends to be confused with consciousness *per se*. This then leads us to think that this limited feature is the whole mind.

The second step of learning is also structured by a further unfolding of meaning. In this instance it is a transformation involving *explicit to explicit* meaning. These kinds of transformations occur in the interactions of signs and symbols and they represent a 'head' or academic form of knowledge and what is often categorized as a rational mode of understanding. This kind of knowledge, with its emphasis on explicit meaning, is highly prized by those who believe in reason and rationality. The rational view of the world can be reinforced by the idea that the conscious mind is all there is to mind. Yet this view deletes much, for what is missing from the dictates of reason are usually the implicit contexts of mind that underpin and support the distinctions and differences of *explicit to explicit* exchanges.

The final step of learning within the ordinary mind is structured by those transformations from *explicit to implicit* meaning. With these transformations, meaning begins to *enfold*, in contrast to the earlier steps that have unfolded meaning. With this third step, from *explicit to implicit*, meaning begins to be enfolded through processes that unify and contextualize the differences that have been established through the earlier steps of identification and differentiation. The final step of becoming unifies, contextualizes and integrates distinctions. Such holistic integration of mind is achieved when we place a value and emphasis on the role, depth and fecundity of implicit meaning.

In summary, the three learning steps of becoming transform the codes of meaning in the following manner:

Implicit to explicit;
Explicit to explicit; and
Explicit to implicit.

There is a fourth transformation of meaning, which is distinct from the other three steps in the arc of learning. This is the transformation from *implicit to implicit* meaning. These are the changes that occur with intuition, insight and realization. Such transformations act as bridges between the cosmic mind of the Host and the ordinary mind of the individual. These kinds of transformations also act as the underlying support field within which each of the other three steps of becoming operates. *Implicit to implicit* exchanges also operate between individuals and in this form they are usually called extra-sensory perception.

Knowledge
The three learning steps of *identification, differentiation and integration* can also be understood as steps for acquiring credible knowledge. All knowledge involves us in dealing with differences in some way. For example, the first step of identification involves creating differences and distinctions through the recognition and identification of things. With the second step of differentiation we extend our ability to create, sort and refine differences into finer distinctions and greater degrees of differentiation. Celebrated and unchecked, this second step of learning is likely to result in the chaos of unlimited differentiation, a by-product of which will be a series of false divisions within the mind and, ultimately, the fragmentation of our knowledge. The third step of learning integrates the differences and distinctions

created by the two former steps. Acquiring credible knowledge is therefore only possible at the final step of learning where order is created through the processes of contextualizing multiple distinctions. Context always provides order for any series of distinctions and differences.

It should come as no surprise that when the first two learning steps are relied upon to produce credible knowledge they fail to do so because of their inherent limitations. In general, when we base our judgments, opinions or behavior on patterns of identification we will be jumping to premature conclusions or reacting emotionally. This is because patterns and syndromes of identification form our emotional life. While these patterns can provide us with a motivating force that can drive us to undertake difficult tasks, these patterns of identification are essentially untrustworthy. The reason why the first step of identification is untrustworthy is because it contains the logic of identity: of A equals B.

This logic is based upon a connection (by identification) of an explicit A with an explicit B. This order may seem irrational or even illogical but it is the first essential step in learning anything. It is the first step, for example, that enables infants to learn that the form of their mother (A) equals maternal/secure feelings (B) that will in later life be called maternal love. Hence the processes of identification are about identifying two or more distinctions as if they are one. This limiting ordering represents the necessary first step in learning anything. However, this kind of limited knowledge is not dependable when we use it to construct opinions, conclusions or behavior, yet using patterns of identification is a common practice in contemporary society and one that is reinforced by modern media, marketing and consumer strategies that play on our desires as well as extending them.

In terms of the second step of differentiation, the drawback to this kind of knowledge is that while this kind of knowledge is much more expansive than the closed and bonding order of identification it is nevertheless limited. This kind of thinking has a focus on details of various differences and distinctions but this view neglects the broader contexts. Knowledge produced by the second step of learning thus tends to ignore implicit meaning while over-valuing explicit details and the rational logic of explicit details. The result of this kind of focused differential thinking is that these differences become separations that divide and this kind of fragmentation leads to the compartmentalisation of our mind. This kind of knowledge gives rise to arguments and rational justifications and is also liable to provide us with a single instrumental view of reality. The negative by-products of this kind of chaos-based knowledge are stress, anxiety, fear, anger, blame and a sense of injustice.

The idea that God as a super-personality dispenses justice is therefore, a consequence of thinking that has not progressed beyond the second stage of differentiation. This kind of thinking is very much part of the human condition and a feature of the ordinary mind and as a result is not part of the Host context: the Spirit Supreme. As I have said, when we blame God for the suffering in the world our blame automatically inhibits our capacity to learn. In other words, our rational arguments against God's injustices do not take into account the broader context in which these arguments arise, and this context is the ordinary mind. When this context is addressed directly it becomes clear that linking justice to divine Providence is an unreliable feature of the second step of learning.

It is only through the third and final learning step of *integration* that knowledge can be produced that does not have some inbuilt limitations or drawbacks. This is because knowledge produced from the third learning step combines the other two steps of identification and differentiation into something new, coherent and holistic. This integrated knowledge is rooted in context and it comes in the structure of a gestalt. A gestalt of knowledge has a background context that orders all those foreground distinctions that represent the constituent parts of any coherent system. This kind of knowledge represents a holistic wisdom and it provides us with the moral idea of unity within diversity. It is also the kind of wisdom that is displayed in natural ecological systems. In other words, it is the inherently holistic knowledge of Nature. This third learning step of becoming is also a mode of thought, which I call empathy.

The movement from the second step of *differentiation* to the third step of *integration* represents a big change in thinking and learning. This is a transformation that goes from rational and logical arguments into the broader context of infinite love. One example of this change is our concept of God. A God with a super-personality is created by rational and differential minds, which separate us from this super-personality who may or may not be just. Such thinking derives from logical argument but is almost wholly closed off to learning. In contrast, God as love is created by empathetic minds, which connect the ordinary minds of people to the beloved Meaning within. The relationship between the Beloved within and our ordinary mind is closer than a heart beat for it is the sight within seeing. Integrated, empathetic thinking thus opens us to learn from each other but also more importantly, opens us to learn from the Beloved within.

We can now answer the question of how justice relates to the Beloved within by saying that while there is no super-personality that is just, there is a close and equal relationship between everyone's ordinary mind and the cosmic mind. This is to say that no individual or group stands outside Meaning. In addition, no individual or group has a special, freer and exceptional relationship to the Beloved within than any other group, and that includes the religious groups. This is to say no more than that everyone has a cosmic mind, which is the foundation of his or her ordinary mind. We know this equality of connection in the way a child knows its mother, through the wealth of intuitive meaning that this relationship generates.

I suggest that this equality of connection to the cosmic mind of Meaning is the innate basis for all justice systems that demand equality before the law. Justice systems are based upon a sense of fairness that comes from the idea that everyone is equal. We are equal, even though each of us is unique, by having the infinite and divine Host as the basis of our ordinary minds. This is an equal and holographic relationship in that the whole is reflected in every part and each part is a unique feature that makes up the fabric of the whole.

Chapter 6 – Watchout for Whiteouts

The weather patterns of the ordinary mind arise out of the meanings that swirl around the second, third and fourth levels of the fourfold self. These circular eddies are therefore established by the contexts of bodily activity, through collective actions, and by our use of symbols. The three contexts of the ordinary mind are as follows:

The ordinary mind:

    4 – Symbol –abstract forms
    3 – Culture – collective habits
    2 – Body –concrete forms

In this chapter I want to discuss how the swirls of the ordinary mind create the whiteout of illusions so that we see reality falsely. How do we tell the difference between illusions and reality? An illusion is considered to be a false perception, whereas reality it taken to be a perception that is true. In terms of Meaning, illusions arise from closed systems while truth is constituted by open systems that allow meaning to be easily transformed and learning to take place. It follows then that a closed system of meaning represents a false conclusion, opinion or judgment, while an open provisional system creates a truth by mirroring how meaning is made and transformed.

This question about illusions and reality has customarily been answered by relating it to knowledge or awareness. For example, a common metaphor in Eastern philosophy for explaining the difference between reality and illusion is that of the rope and the snake. In the dark we may see a rope and mistake it for a snake. When there is enough light we realize that it was only a rope, and the snake disappears. Given the light of spiritual awareness we can tell the difference between the illusion of a snake and the reality of the rope.

Whatever the story we use to make the distinction between illusion and reality, the central issue of the question comes back to our vision. The three vertical levels of the ordinary mind (*symbols, culture and body*) combine to create our vision or perception of the world. Illusions are created around and through these three levels. What happens on each of these levels can create closed illusionary systems of meaning that reduce our vision and restrict our ability to learn. The ordinary mind is very good at creating whiteouts from closed systems of meaning that restrict our learning. For example, when these three levels of mind are combined we may create the big whiteout about our assumed autonomy and see ourselves as autonomous independent agents with private minds and having a separate identity of ego.

However, the ordinary mind often does not make meaning in harmony with the open nature of Meaning and we commonly create whiteouts by using closures of meaning, such as the idea of having free will. Yet how is it possible for the ordinary mind to create illusions by making meaning if the structure of Meaning is always open? In other words, how is it possible to go against the nature of Meaning?

It should be remembered that meaning is not made by pulling on mechanical levers and nor is it made by a free agent in a private capacity. Both these simplistic ideas do not take account of the nature of Meaning itself. Rather, we see the world and make sense of it by using symbols within a cultural context and through our bodily activities. These three levels of the ordinary mind are not autonomous and nor are they separate from each other. Yet while they are integrated at the same time they are distinct from each other and from the cosmic mind of the Host.

Their autonomy or agency is therefore relative to the whole and this means that overall the ordinary mind has only a relative agency or a relative freedom of choice. Because of this relative agency we are able to be creative in finding new and different connections for old situations. The down side of this creativity is that we often close meanings that are actually open and when we do this the overall relative autonomy of the ordinary mind tends to appear as absolute.

One point to note here is that illusions are only ever created by the ordinary mind and not by the cosmic mind of the Host. Let us look at the habits we use to create some conventional whiteouts within the three levels of the ordinary mind.

Symbols

Humility is the foundation of all other virtues, so said Saint Augustine. Humility comes from knowing your-self. A good place to begin to know your-self is to study how language works because language is a context of mind. It is the most abstract level of the ordinary mind. This context involves the symbols of language, measurement, mathematics, money, and as well every sign or object we use to signify something.

The context of language has a relative agency in that meaning is simultaneously both hidden and revealed by it. This contradictory function comes into operation whenever we speak, write or use symbols to communicate. It tells us that for every expression, message, measurement, signal or text we use something is revealed while at the same time some accompanying meaning is hidden.

This contradictory agency of language makes it impossible to express a concise, clear, logical and certain statement without ambiguity or uncertainty. In other words, every statement will always be provisional and contain ambiguities and uncertainties. This is the case even for mathematics and logic.

The failure of language to ever produce a total closed certainty is due to its representational role as well as its status within the mind. Language occupies the most abstract level of mind and therefore can only ever operate by pointing to non-symbolic events that exist prior to this level of abstraction. The only time this is not the case is when language deliberately or implicitly point to itself (as I am doing here).

The role of language is always relative and representational and as a consequence, all information, data, measurements and stories will be provisional and open to the vagaries of cultural change and different interpretations. Open-ended uncertainty is therefore, the reality of language use and also the profile of humility.

Yet most of us will ignore how the symbols we use simultaneously reveal as well as conceal meaning. A common attitude is to treat them like the reflection in a mirror or even to see language as having no agency, as neutral in respect to the way we express ourselves or how our mind works.

Such trust leads to a sense of pride that comes with the illusion of certainty. This happens because we believe in the veracity of a single meaning. Whenever we want to create the illusion of certainty we resort to the use of the single meaning, which is created by a closed and unambiguous statement. The illusion of the certainty generated by closed statement represents the sleep of single vision; the outward sign of ignorance and pride.

The sleep of single meaning comes often from a literal and surface reading or rendering of any text, whether scientific, religious, ethnic, commercial or monetary. As a consequence of disregarding the relative agency of language we end up being dominated by symbols, that is, we unintentionally give symbols absolute control over our thoughts. Dominated by language is to be rigid and fixed in our thought patterns, it is to live in the prison-house of language.

The meaning we make through the use of language is always

uncertain, yet we often dismiss this uncertainty in favor of the precise sequential logic of reason or measurement, fact or data. It is then we will find ourselves out of tune with the essential nature of meaning itself. When we are out of tune with the reality of meaning we can easily be lulled by spin, rhetoric and advertising.

Out of tune with the structure of meaning is to believe that something is absolute when it is actually relative. This reversal of the order within the mind can easily occur whenever we over-value the explicit details of measurements, money, logic or empirical data and disregard the wider contexts in which these details always occur. When we see the world through this kind of view it is very limited and narrow. In the words of the Zen Master Yoka Daishi (665–713), we should not belittle the sky by looking through a pipe.

Perhaps a productive way to discuss language is through the use of metaphor. In this regard language can be seen as a house. As a general principle, everyone should become literate and to be able to live in the house of language and use this abstract level of their mind with some dexterity. If we live illiterate lives and only vaguely know about the house of language we will suffer from the harsh weather conditions of an inhospitable social climate as well from as a lack of maturation and fulfillment.

On the other hand, if we are fascinated by the wonders of sign and symbol we may find we are unable to leave this house. If this happens, (as it so often does with tertiary-trained people) the symbols we use become our prison-house. In the prison-house of language there are few outside views, with no distant perspective that shows us the limitations of what we are saying or the values we have given to money and status. Hence, there will be no other reality than the one created by this 'pipe-view'.

It is therefore essential to be able to leave the house of language. But how do we leave? We do not leave by simply denying that this level of mind has agency. This is the ploy used by materialists who simply delete any reference to language, mind or meaning in their investigations. Neither can we leave by living in rags in a cave or by taking a vow of silence in a monastery. Such practices have a range of practical, spiritual benefits but they do not automatically guarantee an escape from the prison-house of language. This prison house can often manifest itself as the 'monkey mind' in meditation.

Rather, we leave this house through the humble doorways that sub-text, context, metaphor, irony and parable offer us. These are the practical passports to a freedom beyond the self-enclosed walls of pride and the prison-house of the single vision. These are the escape passages that lead us into the light of a larger and perhaps fourfold vision, a vision that comes from the non-symbolic depth of spirit and meaning.

Metaphors are used to express a depth of meaning. A depth of meaning also signifies and records the multi-levels of mind. We therefore, need to employ metaphors in order to escape from the prison-house of the single meaning. One example would be to reduce the house of language to the size of a cartographer's toolbox. A cartographer is a mapmaker and in this sense we are all cartographers for symbols are a map-making (representational) mode of thought. Symbols provide us with maps of, and for, other territories. Map-making is itself a metaphor that highlights the important distinction between the map and the territory.

There can be many maps of the same territory and usually the more maps the more meaning that is revealed. This implies that no single map is ever complete, unconditional or has an absolute and closed value. Maps are always works-in-progress. Even the axiomatic and factual maps of science or even the sacred 'maps' of Holy Scripture represent maps that are incomplete and open to interpretation. This is the case even for the word of God, for such words have to be read and understood by ordinary fallible minds. Hence, the humble truths we create by using language, discourse and symbols cannot be anything other than interim, provisional and incomplete.

The great Russian scientist, Ivan Petrovich Pavlov called our language capacity the 'second signal system' and declared that its use by humans makes us distinct from other animals. However, when we take this context of mind for granted, or pay little attention to how it conceals as well as reveals meaning, then our responses will tend to imitate the habitual conditioning responses of animals. It is then we will begin to live stressful lives dominated by the whiteouts of single visions.

Culture

According to Professor Robert Putnam the average American is very religious yet remarkably tolerant. (ABC Radio, 'Religion and Ethics', 20/06/12) This coincidence of tolerance and religiosity is apparently unusual in human societies. Putnam suggests that the growth of college education has damaged biblical literalism but he does point to other factors at work in the culture, like building personal connections across group boundaries that has made the average American more tolerant.

Like humility, tolerance is a virtue and it comes from building meaningful links across social and religious divisions. One way to begin to learn how to build these connections is to understand something about your own culture.

Culture is a context of your mind. It is a context of mind that has relative agency and this agency relates to what could be called our 'swarm intelligence'. 'Swarm intelligence' is a term used to describe the in-flight maneuvers of birds or the co-coordinated activities in beehives or termite mounds. The mind is made entirely of relations of meaning and these are essentially communal and therefore, there is a strong innate force working on us to live as we truly are: as an integrated part of a lager collective.

As a member of a cultural group we share with others members all kinds of unspoken, implicit understandings about what is important and how to live our lives. These shared cultural understandings are supported by a deeper framework of meaning of which our ordinary minds are a part. For example, when we communicate with others the exchanges we make are constructed from a medium that has already been given to us. This is the spiritual medium of meaning.

If this were not the case and each person made only his or her own private meaning then there would be no basis for exchanging meaning, or shared understandings or any communication at all. Every communication exchange, even those across different languages, begins by sharing a common set of pre-conscious understandings about the implicit and explicit conditions of meaning. The mythological Tower of Babel story that tells us how separate we are, is entirely false. Every communication exchange no matter how small has the same coherent and unifying foundation of meaning within meaning.

Owen Barfield has argued that our collective representations tend to constitute 'the world we all accept as real'.[1] The 'real' is what we consider to be the norm; the predictable and acceptable world in which social behavior is judged, rewarded or punished. The real world of our swarm intelligence is usually not an open, conditional place of cultural relativity. Yet the cultural context of the ordinary mind occupies a small and relative place with the structure of mind. And because this context is relative it cannot answer to the absolute demands of 'the real'. Being relative, the realities that are constructed by our norms of behavior are also relative. To believe otherwise is to believe in the illusion that you and your culture are exceptional or superior.

The linguist Benjamin Lee Whorf had a similar view. Whorf was famous in the twentieth century for his principle of 'linguistic relativity'. Whorf studied the language habits of Native Americans, such as the Hopi and Shawnee, and compared these with Indo-European ones or what he called Standard Average European (SAE). What Whorf meant by the principle of linguistic relativity was that 'all observers are not led by the same physical evidence to the same picture of the universe, unless their linguistic backgrounds are similar, or can in some way be calibrated'.²

This principle of linguistic and cultural relativity means that no one is free to describe the environment with absolute impartiality. Different cultures will therefore view the world differently and this difference will depend upon the predisposition that underpins the culture or sub-culture. For example, in a tribal culture the overall bonds of the tribe are those that center on the inclusion of its members and the exclusion of 'other' non-tribal people. When this happens for an entire group of people their patterns of cultural identification become so strong that the bonding of their norms and swarm intelligence largely remain unquestioned, subliminal and habitual.

A tribal culture does not have to have members who carry spears and live in mud huts. A modern-day tribe can have members who belong to an exclusive church, mosque, club or society, send their children to exclusive schools and have them worship in exclusive ways. In terms of meaning making, a tribe is a culture group based largely upon the learning processes of identification and having members who share the normative values of 'in' and 'out' groups. When we identify with a modern-day tribal culture this double identification of them and us creates customs and norms of behavior that carry exclusive values and serious threats of excommunication for those who fall outside the norms of the tribe. For the religious tribe, heaven is only available to the tribe's members and not to outsiders.

In contrast, when a society's norms rest largely upon the meaning making of divisions and separations of language it produces the contemporary world of science and technology. Such a society has values that come from a focus on differences to such a degree that they (the differences) become ends rather than the means for solving problems. When differences are over-valued they multiply and turn into separations that divide. A cultural orthodoxy based upon divisions and separations is one that fragments knowledge and social interactions through the dogmas of individualism, materialism, rationalism, realism and positivism.

The hallmark of a fragmented society represents the culture of Reason (with a capital 'R') and while this regime of meaning is definitely a step away from tribal culture it is not a full step away when it comes to cultural identity and knowing who we are. This is to say that while much of our modern culture of Reason relies upon the foundation principle of differentiation for solving life's problems, when it comes to our sense of who we are we tend to revert to tribal thinking and the bonding processes of identification.

In other words, we will tend to identify with the underlying norms of a tribal culture. As our modern culture of Reason has a linguistic predisposition to name objects rather than contexts or events it has the consequent tendency to prescribe us as objects, that is, as private, solo and separate entities.

Within our modern culture of Reason, mainstream materialism has constructed a 'real' material world that appears independent from the processes of observation. Hence our collective habits are also a collective forgetting. What the materialist forgets is the relative agency of his culture. Like the fiction writer who tells a story from the omnipotent point of view, the materialist scientist has tended also to assume an omnipotent point of view. Unlike most fiction writers, scientists do not normally take into account their own language and cultural contexts. Yet scientists cannot escape the relativity of their culture simply by assuming their theories and experiments are beyond the culture in which they work.

The creation of a positivistic world is based on the infallibility of the mechanical scientific method and it is continually constructed by exchanging abstractions like money and information. At the core of this real world is scientific measurement, which means that the unreal represents that which is un-measurable and non-computational. God is therefore unreal because He is un-measurable, but then so also is meaning, mind, culture, language, intuition, realization and insight unreal. The effects of these erasures are many.

Barfield refers to these kinds of forgetting as the making of idols. An idol is made when the relative status of a representation is forgotten and it becomes instead a 'real' and unqualified reality. This is also a description of an illusion. Communities that create the 'real' world of idols suffer from the idolatry. Idolatry therefore tends to be a collective forgetting. However, a collective illusion is a state of mind that not only refers to some primitive forms of religious worship; it also describes many common aspects of scientific thought and practice.

In distinction from tribal culture and cultures of reason there is the culture of empathy. While empathy is yet to become a widespread collective response in any society there are many individuals in every society whose way of life and mode of thought are predominantly empathetic. For the person of empathy what is real are the connections he or she has with others. For the empathetic person interpersonal relationships are more real and more important than any tribal pronouncement that divides the world into them and us. The importance of interpersonal relationships represents the earthly feature of real spiritual exchanges with the divine presence of the Spirit within.

An empathetic culture takes language into account but only as the metaphoric part of a wider non-symbolic reality. A metaphoric understanding is necessary to understand allegory, parable, irony and satire and is therefore quite distinct from an either/or tribal view of the world and also different from the positive literalism of Reason. An empathetic culture takes itself as relative to other cultures and perspectives. In addition, from an empathetic culture a mature spirituality can grows. This is the mind that makes meaning by discerning differences yet can make out their necessary connections within wider contexts. This is the fourfold vision of the poet, William Blake.

In summary, how tolerant we are relates to how well we understand the biases of our own culture. If we accept without question the predispositions of our culture then we are unlikely to show tolerant to those different from us. Under these forgetful conditions our reactions will tend towards a two-valued, 'black or white' tabloid view of the world where we identify the good, reasonable and familiar as extensions of ourselves, while the strange or different as foreign and 'other.' A tabloid and tribal appreciation will tend towards a hard-edged, black or white, idol-worshipping forgetfulness.

A second response involves a materialistic morality, which dismisses out of hand any implication of an underlying spiritual context in the universe. Finally, there is a more empathetic and disclosing cultural view that admits to the absolute value of social connections while accepting the relative status of other cultural positions. Finally the culture of empathy accepts the great dream of life dreamt by the One numinous cosmic consciousness; the prime cause from which all other causes radiate.

Body
The body context represents the last level of the ordinary mind. This context is as conditional and relative as the other two levels. The agency of the physical body is therefore also relative. It is on this point that materialists disagree and instead of viewing the physical body as having a relative agency they see its material state, along with the rest of the physical world, as the causal source for all exchanges. This is true for common materialism, which constructs the illusion of the 'ego' as well as for the theoretical materialism that underpins much of Western medical science.

A common Western understanding of the term 'ego' is that it represents the conscious subject, or the real self of the individual. In terms of Eastern philosophy, the ego is the false self. In terms of Meaning, Eastern philosophy is correct: the ego is a false self because it is an illusion. The rationale for this conclusion goes like this: there is nothing within the laws and conditions of Meaning that indicates the possibility of separations, splits or divisions. As the Western idea of ego is based upon the assumption that it represents a separate entity this idea is in conflict with the laws of Meaning. In addition, when we identify the three levels of the ordinary mind (symbols, culture and body) together into one identity the result is the ego. And when we identify the relative autonomy of the three levels the result is an autonomous ego. In terms of Meaning, the individual is unique not because of a unique identity (ego) but because of how the three levels of the ordinary mind interact together and with the cosmic Host context. The Western meaning of ego as the true self is therefore a whiteout: an illusion.

When it comes to considering the body most of us never progress much beyond the first learning step of identification. Stuck in this process we identify the body as the self; this is the entity we think we are. In addition, we tend to endow this separate and solo identity with the power of a self-generating agency, that is, with an autonomy that comes from our will or intention. Disguised in this way we believe that we are the doer and controller of things and that 'my' autonomous ego has the capacity to 'own' objects like cars, houses and sometimes other people. This series of whiteouts is sustained and supported by the contemporary global culture in which most of us live. It is also reinforced by the use of a categorical language (for example, the identificational verb 'to be') that produces the certainty and superficiality of a single vision. At this point we are six feet under the snow but believe we really are free as birds in the sky.

The relative agency of the body can perhaps be best understood by thinking of the body as an instrument, a physical instrument through which the intelligent energy of Meaning flows. It is an instrument like a flute in that it does not create music (meaning) but simply plays a variety of tunes that are best suited to the physical structure of the instrument.[3] As an instrument the body can play several kinds of tunes: i) it can play songs of dissonance and disharmony; or ii) songs of harmony, compassion and love.

Most of the songs of disharmony begin with patterns of identification associated with the body. This is the ego tune, which in effect says: 'I am this body.' As a consequence of this common materialistic error we think of ourselves as alive when the body is active and then expect to die when the body dies. Such songs confound us about who we are and what is in our best interests. These songs contribute to our misery, hatred, blame, jealousy, envy, greed, war and a difficult death. Some short-term pleasures may result from these songs, which can fulfill our immediate desires, but this kind of singing usually comes with a good deal of grief and suffering.

Grief and suffering are some of the emotions many of us will go through when faced with the prospect of dying. In her groundbreaking research with terminally ill patients, Elisabeth Kubler-Ross identified five stages of dying.[4] These are:

- Denial (this isn't *happening* to me!)
- Anger (why is this happening to *me*?)
- Bargaining (I promise I'll be a better person *if...*)
- Depression (I don't *care* anymore)
- Acceptance (I'm *ready* for what comes).

In her book *On Death and Dying* Kubler-Ross tells how her research developed in Billings Hospital at the University of Chicago. At first many physicians were critical of her interviews with dying patients, claiming the process 'exploited' vulnerable patients. However, by 1967 she had largely won over the doctors and was conducting unorthodox but popular weekly seminars. In *On Death and Dying* she describes the different stages of dying in psychiatric terms as defense mechanisms or coping mechanisms. These stages are now widely called the stages of grief and are used in grief support and counseling.

What is taken for granted in the five stages of dying is the Western idea that we have a solo mind, which is identified with a particular physical body. In other words, death of the body is assumed to be the 'end' or the 'loss' of us. What we at first deny, then get angry, bargain and then become depressed about is the impending loss or the end of who we are. If we believe we are our body with a private and solo mind then dying is a miserable affair. Even in the final stage of acceptance there is no joy. Kubler-Ross says that if a patient is helped to work through the previous stages (that is, helped with the learning associated with these stages) 'he will reach a stage during which he is neither depressed nor angry about his "fate" '.[5] Accordingly the patient will have 'mourned the impending loss of so many meaningful people and places and he will contemplate his coming end with a certain degree of quiet expectation'. However, acceptance is not 'OK' or a happy stage, but a kind of 'void of feelings'.

While this five-stage model developed out of the 1960s interviews with dying patients in Chicago there is no underlying thread or theory that ties these stages together or places them within a wider context. The wider context that perhaps could link these stages coherently is the context of Meaning, which involves the arc of learning with its three steps of *identification, differentiation and integration*. Unlike many situations that we are able to put off for another day, being told you have a terminal illness forces you to re-evaluate your life and as a consequence plunges you into a learning process associated with that re-evaluation. If that re-evaluation begins with the identification, 'I am my body' then there is a long way to go before reaching a more integrated and holistic state of mind.

Even though the reality of dying does not allow much room to resist the learning associated with this inevitable event, the stages of denial, anger, bargaining and depression are patterns of identification associated with grief and connected to a sense of loss. For those who still believe they are the body, the fifth and final stage of dying offers no release but represents a 'void of feelings'. I suggest that Kubler-Ross' five stages of dying are culturally relative and therefore represent the five stages of dying for those Western individualists who believe they have a solo mind and that their private mind is part of the body that dies. Such belief systems represent songs of disharmony that have their roots in patterns of identification associated with materialism.

The songs of harmony and love are sung by using the full range of notes, for these songs are about the holistic integration of connection and empathy. They tell stories about learning and becoming and they embody uncertain and incomplete pictures that have no final closure or solution. They are sustained by intuitive connections that underpin all sensory differences and by a vision of the big picture; a larger self that is beyond the ego and also beyond the ordinary mind. People who sing these songs, even badly, are likely to experience communion and a level of joy and satisfaction that sustains them through the vicissitudes of life and also through the processes of dying.

I am therefore suggesting that dying need not be the miserable event that the five stages of grief describe but can involve a final stage when connection, love and equanimity are felt by a dying patient. Kubler-Ross even refers to this kind of response in *On Death and Dying* when describing reactions by students to the interviews she uses, and in particular when a student was upset by a dying patient's 'calmness and equanimity'. The student thought the patient was 'faking' it 'because it was inconceivable to him that anyone could face such a crisis with so much dignity.'⁶ I have also experienced a similar state of equanimity in the face of death by close relatives.

In regard to the relativity of the body, this context represents our anchor and orientation point within the physical, empirical world. The incarnate body thus provides us with the scientific notion of 'locality'. In this sense the body locates us within the differential grid created by the three dimensions of perceptual space and the one dimension of conceptual time. This sense of locality comes with an expectation that the world in which we live has an inbuilt asymmetrical and clockwise causality. This is the notion that prior causes always have effects that come later in time. (The metaphor of clockwise causality is often accompanied by the metaphor of the arrow of time even though these metaphors conflict with each other). As to the question of difference between what scientists call objective space and time and what psychologists call perceptual space and conceptual time, the answer is: there is none. Objective space and time are simply scientific terms for what in essence is the consciousness of perceptual space and conceptual time.

Our specific location within space and time is also relative, but not in terms of the speed of light as Einstein proposed in his theories of relativity; the speed of light is a measurement and hence a derivative product of our concept formations. Our specific location in space and time is relative to the non-local eternity of the Host context. Yet the body's specific yet relative locality also tends to provide a cruel reinforcement for the identification patterns of the ego. This reinforcement comes about because the ego assumes itself to have the very attributes that the body has: a specific, differential and separate locality in space and time. As the ego assumes these attributes to be unqualified there is a sense of absolute loss when faced with the prospect of dying. The ego thus sets up the conditions for us to suffer and feel grief in the face of death. However, when the body is understood to be relative to the eternity of the Host context the ego has a much more difficult job loading us up with the identification patterns of grief and suffering.

The body's conditional status therefore relates to its location as relative to the foundation Host context: the meaning of Meaning. The body's location within the four contexts of mind places it as the last context of the ordinary mind but also the first context through which meaning begins to unfold from the implicitness of the Host context. In addition, the secondary and relative status of the body means that the physical nature of the body along with its various systems do not originate thought, nor can they organize the body's birth, its patterns of growth, development or death. The body's relative autonomy is thus created out of the union of three distinct influences: i) the Meaning coming from the Host context; ii) the meaning coming from the ordinary mind; and iii) the meaning that the body's systems generate when the environment interacts with the body's genetic makeup. The interacting influences of these three factors means that while there is a high level of complexity related to the meaning of this context, the overall effect of these influences is to qualify and relativize the status and autonomy of the body.

An example of this relative status comes from Zen Buddhism that tells us, 'Things do not have their own nature'.[7] This means that the body is not self-caused, nor is it a self-organized system. Its nature has been given and continues to be given in the stream of Meaning that flows through it and makes it pulsate with the vitality we call life. The incarnate body is therefore an instrument, an organic form through which meaning is made, transformed and channeled. The body is like a flute in the hands of the master flute player. Because of this dependency we can ask of the body, 'what does a flute know about music'?[8] Or, a similar question from the point of view of science: 'what do the cells know about the overall blueprint that arranges the body's form, its morphogenesis'? On this question Rupert Sheldrake has written that while our DNA can make the protein bricks that build the body, the body's master plan is not contained in these bricks.[9] Thus the protean bricks, of which the body is made, have only a relative agency; they do not and cannot act as the autonomous agency that constructs the body's plan and its blueprint. This point concerning biological relativity has been largely ignored or erased by Western medical science.

During its lifetime a body grows, develops, and then begins to decline and die. These physical developmental changes affect the way we mentally respond to our environment. For example, at fifteen our response to the environment will be different from our responses at the age of thirty, fifty and seventy. In the manner that it affects our mental life, the body's physical development represents part of the relative agency of the body. The combination of these normal physical and mental changes represents maturation processes or maturation stages. In terms of Meaning, there are three maturation stages which we pass through and which are associated with the three learning steps of the ordinary mind (*identification, differentiation and integration*).

The first maturation period associated with identification spans approximately the first twenty years of life. The second (associated with differentiation) covers the next twenty years and the maturation period of integration accounts for the rest of life. By bringing together the three steps of learning with the corresponding maturation periods in the life of the individual we have the following matrix:

identification	-	the first 20 – 25 years;
differentiation	-	from 20 to 40 years;
integration	-	from 40 years onwards

In this first twenty years of life we begin our long maturation and development journey towards a more mature consciousness.

Identification is the beginning step in all learning, no matter how old we are. In the first twenty years, however, we often mistakenly take this first learning step to be the final and mature conclusion of things. When this happens we jump to all kinds of premature conclusions about a variety of life's problems, but especially about who we are and what we like.

The maturation stage of differentiation spans approximately the next twenty years (from twenty through to about forty). It is in this period that we begin to master the social and cultural differentiations that for twenty years we have slowly been moving towards. This can be a period of high performance and expertise in our chosen field.

The third and final stage of maturation is associated with integration. When we reach mid-life the development of our consciousness turns naturally towards valuing integration and feelings of empathy. This turn of events can often cause a crisis in our life, a life that has grown used to all the division and separations that a finely tuned intellect can create in a modern community. The mid-life crisis that eventually ends in a more integrated, mature and harmonious life is a common feature in contemporary society.[10]

In addition to the growth and development of the body, its location within the four contexts of mind situates it as a field of interactions between two poles; that is, the relative and local pole of the ordinary mind and the absolute and non-local of cosmic consciousness. The interactions between these two poles are carried out by those meaning exchanges that are overwhelmingly implicit and pre-reflective. These are the exchanges we commonly call visceral sensations, intuitions, realizations and insights. In terms of meaning, these exchanges are *implicit to implicit* exchanges while the kind of knowing these exchanges engender is overwhelmingly implicit knowing. I have more to say about intuition in Chapter 10.

In summary, the ordinary mind, which involves the three

levels of: i) symbols, ii) culture, and iii) the body, is able to create a wide range of illusions and then to believe them to be true. This astonishing ability retards our maturation as well as our rate of learning to such an extent that many of us may never progress past the first learning step of identification. Persistent identification patterns condemn us to live perpetually in a state of whiteout, which is a state of ignorance that denies us the natural benefits that come with a fulfilled life and peaceful death.

Chapter 7 – The Valley of Desires

When I was ten years old the mythical adventures of Jason and the Argonauts sparked the fires of my young imagination. At home we had a book about the Argonauts that my mother read out loud to us. I also remember listening to a radio program in the afternoons called the Argonauts. So one way or another the adventures of these ancient mythical characters became a staple part of my early childhood. I used to ask my mother if these stories about the Argonauts were true and she would say they were myths, which seemed to mean that they could be true but we were not sure. These stories, however, were always told in a literal manner, as if the author were reporting real events. They were, in effect, literal myths.

A literal myth flirts with our imagination but then suggests we should pay little attention to the imagined. A literal myth also changes a cautionary tale about the difficulties of becoming into an action-packed adventure. A literal rendering of a myth will also change metaphoric characters into everyday ones. When this happens we can get misogynist stories. This is what happened to me with the Argonaut story of the Sirens. In our children's book there was a picture of three beautiful, scantily clad young women standing on a rocky outcrop overlooking the sea. These beauties were making enticing gestures to a nearby sailing ship full of eager-looking sailors. The story that accompanied this image was about these three beautiful Sirens who sang and played bewitching music so that any passing sailors were in danger of being enticed towards them with the result that their ships crashed onto the rocks and the sailors drowned in the sea.

The literal message of the Siren myth is a warning for young men to avoid the enticements of beautiful women who may wreck your life. This is one negative effect of the literal myth. Yet another was my reaction. This cautionary tale did not warn me off the opposite sex, rather it increased my interest in them. For years afterwards I looked for that scantily clad siren that would bewitch me with her beauty and music. And sure enough when I finally found her in my early twenties, I drowned painfully in a sea of romantic unrequited love.

Literal myths tend to destroy the metaphoric multi-layering of meaning within any story. This is what happened with my youthful understanding of the Siren story. This three-thousand-year old story is perhaps more accurately read as a metaphor of the inner journey, or trekking that we can take through the big picture, and the difficulties of becoming a mature and fully developed person. Read like this the Sirens do not represent enticing young women; rather, they are our own desiring impulses that arise within our minds. Read in this manner, the Siren story has something to offer women as well as men. Such a reading also places the emphasis more accurately on inner transformations and the need to change our habits of thought without resorting to blaming others for our own desires. The valley of desires represents one of the territories to be explored up ahead.

In terms of Meaning there are four modes of thought, so there are four possible ways of changing our patterns of thinking and of becoming. Three of these modes are associated with the three steps of learning: *identification, differentiation and integration*. The fourth mode represents the implicit background field within which the other three modes operate.

To discuss these modes of thought in terms of Meaning is a very different enterprise from discussing thought from a psychological or biological point of view. From the point of view of biology (the viewpoint of most western medical science) the mind originates in the brain and is manifest in thought, perception, emotion, will, memory and imagination. These latter terms are considered to be largely irrelevant to the physical processes of the brain that are affected by electrical and chemical processes. A more extreme materialist position is taken in neuroscience where the body and mind are considered as one biophysical system.

Psychological perspectives of the mind place less stress on materialism than the orthodox medical model and have a corresponding emphasis on mental life. This is the position we find in the psychoanalytical model of Sigmund Freud. Freud divided the mind into the unconscious, the preconscious and the conscious. For Freud the conscious mind includes everything that is inside of our rational awareness. Closely allied with the conscious mind is the preconscious and this includes the things that we are not thinking of at the moment but which can easily be drawn into conscious awareness. By contrast, the unconscious mind is a reservoir of repressed feelings, thoughts, urges and memories that are outside of our conscious awareness. Most of the contents of the unconscious are unacceptable or unpleasant to us and represent feelings of pain, anxiety, or conflict.

Freud's categories of conscious and unconscious mind cannot be directly equated with the two conditions of Meaning: implicit and explicit meaning. However, we can say that explicit meaning is always contained within what Freud called the conscious mind. That is to say, the content of the conscious mind is always explicit meaning. In reverse, we can say that since there is no other content to the conscious mind, explicit meaning defines the content and the boundaries of the conscious part of the ordinary mind.

When it comes to the Freudian unconscious there is no clean fit with implicit meaning. This is because the Freudian unconscious mind is like a basement room separate from the conscious mind and, in addition, it represents repressed meaning. By contrast, implicit meaning is an integrated aspect of the conscious, explicit mind, so much so that all explicit meaning is but the surface appearance of underlying implicit contexts. The two conditions of Meaning are therefore far more integrated than Freud's theory of the conscious and the unconscious.

In addition, implicit meaning covers a far greater area than simply the idea of repressed meaning. Implicit meaning may be repressed meaning but it also includes the content of all contexts, not just the contexts of our desires and fears. Perhaps to fill the gaps in his theories Freud coined the term 'un-repressed unconscious'. This is a term that seems to cover much of what we now mean by implicit meaning. However, Freud never clearly developed this concept and it did not play a large part in his work.

In psychological terms we could say that at times implicit meaning is unconscious, that is, repressed meaning associated with desires and fears. However, for most of us implicit meaning does not enter much into our calculations because we are imprisoned in a cultural perspective that has already erased any appreciation of implicit meaning. This is the cultural perspective of Reason; a perspective, which separates out things into binary opposites: rational versus irrational; objective versus subjective, and so on. In this kind of world the implicit is largely ignored, de-valued or erased altogether.

Four Modes

In terms of Meaning, the ordinary mind has four modes of thought, not two or three as suggested by Freud. These four modes arise out of the various kinds of interactions between the two, *implicit* and *explicit* codes of Meaning. Each of these codes is involved in exchanges and each exchange has four possible combinations. These are:

Implicit to implicit;
Implicit to explicit;
Explicit to explicit; and
Explicit to implicit.

The three learning steps of *identification, differentiation and integration* (associated with the ordinary mind) relate to three of these exchanges in the following manner:

identification	**implicit to explicit;**
differentiation	**explicit to explicit;**
integration	**explicit to implicit.**

As for the fourth mode of thought this represents the implicit background field within which the other three modes operate. It involves the *implicit to implicit* exchanges of intuition, insight and realization. I will have more to say about this fourth mode in Chapter 10 where it is called 'innocent love'.

When identification is the dominant feature within a mode of thought in the ordinary mind it tends to be shallow and impulsive, and entails large-scale simplifications. The term that represents thoughts organized by patterns of identification is 'desire'. In contrast, when thoughts are organized around, and oriented to, explicit differences, this mode of thought represents a dry formal intellectualism that we usually describe as being of the 'head' variety. A shorthand title for this mode of thought is 'intellect'. Finally, when thoughts are organized around the integration of differences within larger holistic contexts, this kind of thinking will broaden to include the practices of contemplation and self-enquiry. This is the mode of intelligent compassion or 'empathy'.

The interrelated dynamic of the three modes of the ordinary mind have, therefore, the following features:

Desire	**identification**	**implicit to explicit;**
Intellect	**differentiation**	**explicit to explicit;**
Empathy	**integration**	**explicit to implicit.**

The first point to make about these three modes of thought is that they are not culturally specific but *given*, and so relate to all human behavior in every culture. These three modes of thought represent the basic software language of all ordinary human minds. In comparison to other approaches, these three modes of thought are different from the three degrees of knowledge proposed by Plato. These were: sense-knowledge, geometry, and extra-sensory knowledge or pure intelligence. They are also different from Aristotle's Laws of Thought: identity, non-contradiction and the excluded middle. Aristotle's Laws of Thought have become the basis of western positivist logic and the perspective of materialism that has underpinned much modern scientific theory. In addition, the current model has a slightly different emphasis to the three-mode model proposed by the philosopher, jurist and critic Owen Barfield.[1]

The current four modes of thought give rise to the potentials of exploring the world and understanding who we really are. These four modes also give us the potential for flexibility in how we think. Flexibility is important because how we think determines whether we see the world as friendly, strange or threatening. These different attitudes arise not so much from environmental conditions but from the conditions of thought, that is, from our mode of thinking. A further point is that no one thinks predominantly in the same mode throughout his or her life. This is because these four modes of thought also represent the maturation stages we all pass through in the processes of growth and development (referred to in Chapter 6).

Desire
Identification is the beginning process of learning anything but

if it becomes our general mode of thinking in adult life it will inhibit our ability to learn anything. This inhibition of learning is brought about by circular habits of mind that prevent the other two steps of learning – *differentiation and integration* – from being engaged. A further feature of identificational thinking is that it becomes entangled with the three areas of the ordinary mind: *body, culture and symbols*. Our desires will, therefore, involve our body and the cultural relativities in which we live as well as our expressions. However, our desires will also tend to shy away from engaging directly with those differences that may reduce the power of desire.

Identificational thinking is thinking that becomes fixated on a sense of lack. 'Desire' is a general term for identificational thinking. Within this materialistic culture, the first object of desire is the ego. The ego is the creation of the ordinary mind. It is created by patterns of identification that weld together the three contexts of symbols, cultural habits and expectations and finally the body of the individual. These complex identification patterns produce the simple sense of my self, who I am. The ego is the false self; the true self represents the potentials of the 'I'. The difference between 'I' and 'ego' is the difference between the behavior of the ordinary mind and its essence, which is the cosmic mind of the Host. The mystic poet Kabir (1440–1518) is supposed to have said, 'I am the I within the I'. This can be translated as the sight within the mechanical processes of seeing: I am the sight within the eye and also the 'I' within insight, realization and imagination.

In contrast to the true self of 'I', the ego is an ordinary mind identificational construction that falsifies its own nature. For example, the patterns of identification that create the ego automatically delete its inherent cultural habits and expectations while also erasing the interaction between an individual and community. The ego is then sensed as a free and separate autonomous agency not tied to any community, environment or Divine context. In this materialistic culture we commonly perceive ourselves as separate from others and the evidence that the body is different from others in space and time supports the identificational logic of this conclusion. This sense of a separate and solo 'me' is reinforced by the false idea of an autonomous and independent mind and by behavior that is self-centered, competitive, egotistical or narcissistic.

Some Western psychologists do not agree with these criticisms of the ego, believing instead that most of us have weak or wounded egos that have come about through the results of some kind of trauma or suffering. They believe we should build stronger egos by doing such things as engineering our social environment to support our desires or involving ourselves in competitive activity. Such teachings misunderstand the ego and the difference between the 'I' and the ego. For instance, weak or damaged egos are usually strong egos. The person who is fearful or continually feeling guilty has a very strong ego in the sense that their ego is buttressed by a series of social expectations and defense mechanisms. Guilt and fear rest on the ideal of a separate, autonomous identity that the individual believes to be their true, albeit damaged or threatened nature. In contrast, a truly weak ego comes from a confident and healthy mind and becomes manifest when we let go of control; of our defense mechanisms and desires and let life take its course.[1]

The way a society or groups control their members is by reinforcing identification patterns that create egos; by making people feel guilty, by shame, by fear, by calls to patriotism, by making competition a moral virtue, by reducing meaning through literal imperatives, axiomatic truths or orthodoxies. Each of these control mechanisms reinforces the identification patterns of our desires while making us more dependent and less capable of critical thought. Desire involves the knots of striving (grasping, clinging, wanting) after the lost paradise of connection, love and security. In this sense, desire is an attempt to substitute the open connecting love of our true self with a false identity (the ego) that separates us from others. The tragedy of desire is that it is like a kind of puppetry undertaken by the puppet of the false self: the ego. As such the desires of the ego can never be satisfied because the ego continually points us to a lack and a separation that actually do not exist.

The attraction that is evident in sexual desire is not so much a love for another as the need for connection, a bridge across a gap between our ego and the other. Desire's main preoccupation is not with giving but with taking through the process of identifying with another object. This kind of exchange does not create peace and fulfillment so much as disorder. Caught in the whirlwind of desire we start to believe that we need – and have to have in order to survive – an intense bond with another person. Such lustful desires make us feel lonely and the gravitational pull of attraction to another only seems to relieve that feeling temporarily. Desire is like trying to swim in the swirling turbulence of rapids. The confusion and tumult created by this mode of thought comes from the impossibility of it ever being satisfied.

The vision created by desire is always two-valued and involves the cardinal dualities of subject and object, inner and outer, pain and pleasure. The direction that desire points us in is therefore outwards; hence any outer object can be an object of desire. The French psychoanalyst Jacques Lacan wrote that all desire is the 'desire of the Other'.[2] The object does not have to be a sexual object, although this is common after puberty. Our desires appear to expand our sense of self by becoming attached to objects such as consumer goods and other people. Such objects then become part of 'me'. When we possess or own something the object rightfully becomes part of our ego and therefore 'mine'. In this way I can believe that I own my wife and children as well as my car, camel and goats. This sense of ownership builds on a sense of ego autonomy replete with a sense of personal control and doer-ship.

Learning to unwind the knots of identification in desire and ego is not easy as we are forever looking outwards rather than self-reflectively inwards to the roots of our identificational processes. Desire reinforces our belief in the false self and when desires are not fulfilled we come to believe that we have failed. This sense of failure does not readily recognize that the failed self is actually the inauthentic ego. The sense of failure created by identification patterns can at times become so extreme that this feeling turns into pain or self-harm. Self-harm, whether from razorblades, chains or suicide bombing are activities that reinforce the ego structure. The irony of desire is that we forget who we truly are and, as a consequence, neglect our welfare and long-term interests. This happens even though we may spend more time and energy on our desires than on anything else.

When a social group shares a world-view that is based upon patterns of group identification, the group represents a tribal and/or partisan community. This is also the case for groups who uphold any kind of orthodoxy and in this respect all orthodoxies are essentially tribal. Within tribal regimes the individual's sense of who they are is extended to include the conventional identity of a tribal member. Hence, tribal identity and individual identity are identified as being the same. Tribal regimes can be ancient or modern, religious, ethnic, secular, economic or scientific.

Thinking based upon patterns of identification is also blind. It is blind because the view it has of the world is dominated by a single or binary vision. One way to approach this blindness of desire is through the three learning steps of becoming (*identification, differentiation and integration*). These three learning steps represent the pathway of becoming a holistic and self-reflective authentic person who may come to experience a four-fold vision. Patterns of identification will therefore represent just the beginnings of the truth of a holistic vision. Likewise, the differentiation of the intellect often represents a view devoid of context and therefore less than half the truth of a complete whole. Finally, the integrated vision of empathy represents the complete truth of a fourfold, holistic self-reflective vision. This holistic view is of course a spiritual vision.

On these estimates the thinking mode of desire will always be overwhelmingly blind and ignorant. Desire is blind to most of the meanings in which it is engaged. It is blind to other peoples' world-views, preferences and interests. When we first become infatuated with another we do not see the other person's preferences and interests; all we see is an extension of our own ego. A life lived within this mode of thought is full of reactions, fears, disappointments, blame and misery. Socially this is the disgruntled world of the tabloid media as well as the frantic sales world of advertising and marketing. These days people who suffer from identificational thinking are likely to be dominated by desires manufactured by economic or commercial interests and also generally ignorant of other worldviews and other cultural values. Such ignorance represents a belief that his or her cultural values can and should be generalized to all cultures.

The average adult does not live his or her entire life within this mode of thought, unlike the adolescent or the seriously obsessed. However, desire does act as the magnet, motivation and direction around which most contemporary adults organize their activities. Sympathy is perhaps the most virtuous response that can be generated by our desires. Sympathy is a bonding of like upon like. Sympathy is a reaching out from a base of identificational thinking to include someone else within the normally closed circle of ego and desire. Sympathy is not, however, an empathetic, bridging response that connects and integrates differences in regard to things such as race, religion or ethnicity.

The more common and less virtuous responses that come from our desires are the reactions of greed, envy, anger, lust, pride and jealousy. These are the traditional sins of what is here called, identificational thinking. Elisabeth Kubler-Ross' first three stages of grief: denial, anger and bargaining are also reactions of identification closely associated with our resistance to the loss of desire that goes with a sense of loss of identity. Perhaps the worst reaction that our desires can create is the blind ignorance that prevents us from learning and expanding our vision of the world. This happens in denial and also when we close our minds to the idea that we have a cosmic context of mind: the true self. It also happens when we re-write old legends so they have single meanings that support and reinforce our cultural biases, like those against women.

The patterns of identification that create our desires have little to commend them except for the following: identification is the first learning step in becoming a mature person. This means that to live in this world at all is to create patterns of identification, as these are necessary to learn anything. Therefore our desires cannot simply be denounced as undesirable. A more empathetic response is to speak of them as provisional, as transient, as something to be tolerated in the young but to be left behind as soon as possible.

Yet the difficulty of dissolving one's desires into a mature empathy is the most difficult transformation we can attempt. This change does not result from the common practices of repression, which will only increase their charge and force, nor does it result from the celebration of a libertarian life style. Rather, this transformation out of the valley of desire is enabled only with a serious attempt to become a whole person and assisted by an empathetic master. Such a path will inevitably involve breaking down habitual, closed and painful patterns of identification and then rebuilding them into broader contexts of empathetic compassion. This is the learning task that each of us will, one day, inevitably undertake.

Chapter 8 – Ridges of Intellect

The second mode of thinking for the ordinary mind is based up on the second step of learning and has a focus on differentiation. Thinking based upon differences and differentiation is intellectual thinking. The intellect is a mode of thought that produces detailed and differential knowledge generated by *explicit to explicit* exchanges of meaning. This mode of thought places a great deal of trust in the value and use of symbols (especially language, measurement and money).

Like desire, the intellect represents a transitional stage in learning; it is located at a mid-point in the arc of learning and hence this relative location marks the intellect as a provisional station in the evolution of mind. The intellect's provisional status comes from the place it holds within the arc of learning, lying between desire on the one hand and empathy on the other. This location is relative and therefore conditional on these two modes of thought. The relativity of this location automatically makes the intellect a servant of either desire or empathy as the following figure demonstrates:

Figure 3
Arc of learning

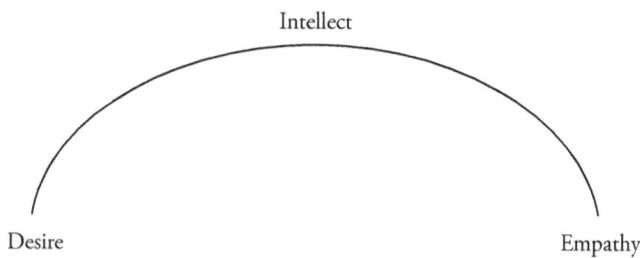

Thus the intellect's inbuilt contradictory tendencies continually point us either forward or backwards in the flow of meaning that is the arc of learning. When the intellect underpins empathy it represents the arguments and distinctions of a larger empathetic picture. In contrast, when the intellect underpins our desires it represents the justification and differences of a small picture that has narrow self-interest, ego and desire at its bottom. The intellect is unable to work on its own behalf, for instance to be more intellectual, because this kind of activity is simply acting on behalf of the ego which is part of our desires. The intellect is therefore always acting, not on its own behalf because that is impossible, but in the service of another mode of thought. Nor can the intellect simply act objectively, for instance, to unselfishly expand the level of scientific knowledge. Again this is an act on behalf of our desires and the ego identity of the individual scientist.

The explicit transformations of the intellect represent a learning tendency that reject the old master narratives of religion and, to a lesser extent, class and caste. However, in this enlightened rejection the intellect can also act on behalf of desire and ego and then it creates its own master narratives of materialism, realism and positivism. The processes of the intellect involve both destruction and construction. These processes revolve around clarifying differences (*explicit to explicit* exchanges) in a manner that destroys old narratives while in the process of building new ones. When the new narrative is successfully accepted so that it exists beyond question it becomes a master narrative or dogma, which is then strongly defended against everything that challenges it. In this manner the narrative of materialism was born, matured and now has become a dogma.

To understand the relativity and biases of the intellect we have to come to terms with the rhetoric of reason. Especially within the last three hundred years the culture of the intellect has often been associated in the West with the ideals and logic of reason. Within the confines of mainstream Western materialism it has been assumed that reason is an unbiased state of mind above the entanglements of self-interest or political expediency. Supporting this idealized status of objectivity is the role played by Aristotelian logic so that when the two are melded into a cultural habit they create an unquestioned expectation that this ideal state of mind exists and is available to the intelligent and reasonable man. The reasonable man, for example, represents the expectation of Western law courts when weighing up evidence in a court hearing. However, this belief and expectation in objective reason is an entirely fallacious assumption based solely upon a materialist rhetoric.

When desire is the master of the intellect the natural learning cycle (*identification, differentiation, integration*) is blocked by the rhetoric of materialism with its appeal to objective reason. Under these regressive conditions the intellect tends to reinforce our desires through the ego agendas we prosecute and the self-interest cases we make. In other words, the intellect is essentially rationalizing our ego desires. In this fashion we can dress them up so they appear less brutal and more socially acceptable. When desire is the master of the intellect we can find logical proof, justification, blame and reasoned argument for almost anything. When this happens the intellect acts like a shady lawyer on behalf of a dodgy client.

When the intellect is servant to the master of desire it employs several strategies to maintain its credibility. Its first strategy is to use language to create splits, separations and divisions where there is actually unity, interconnection and participation. This first strategy can be reinforced by a tertiary education that makes us proficient in the use of fragmentation. When the intellect falls in love with its own ability to differentiate we tend to value differences and differentiation as ideal ends in themselves. When this happens we value *explicit to explicit* exchanges and then call the intellect, Reason with a capital 'R' and give it the status of infallibility, a rank once reserved for the Holy Scriptures. This materialist strategy produces the Tower-of-Babel world where gaps, splits and separations are its most common feature.

The second strategy of the intellect when serving desire is to ignore, erase or devalue contextual and implicit meaning. Intolerance to implicit contextual meaning is a feature of those professional skeptics who create their own certainty by constantly doubting such phenomena as extra sensory perception. Skepticism and doubt represent the comforting reassurance that the Host context and a cosmic order are illusions. The skeptic denies the existence of God, extra-sensory perception, telepathy, ghosts, the memory of water and everything else that seems to challenge the dogmas of a mechanical, explicitly defined rational universe. Amongst the scientific community skeptics have organized themselves into an organization called the Committee for Skeptical Inquiry (CSI) in order to protect mechanical science from backsliding colleagues. In an earlier age the master orthodoxies were more likely to be geographically restricted and based on religion. Historically the critics of all dogmas have been treated harshly. Once they were burnt at the stake or condemned as heretics. Now, under the active influence of skeptics, they simply have their scientific reputations destroyed.

Rational materialism represents the philosophy of the intellect when serving desire. A materialism that is objective and rational is the belief system most revered by mechanical scientists and is held up as the exclusive basis for scientific methods and experiments as well as for the production of all technologies. The image of 'the machine' represents the comforting technological metaphor for what seems to provide science with a future and with the possibility of certainty. A key feature of rational materialism is its general intolerance of uncertainty and the value that is placed on graspable, explicit and differential exchanges that are seen to give rise to our sense of certainty. Uncertainty arises from contextual implicit meaning and it is this kind of ungraspable meaning with which the intellect has difficulties. The intellect's uncertainty of uncertainty was termed by the philosopher theologian, Nicholas of Cusa (1401–1464) as *learned ignorance*.[1] Learned ignorance is a state of the intellect when it *knows it does not know*. When the intellect is confronted by the uncertainties of implicit meaning it has two options: i) it can either accept the ungraspable nature of implicit contextual meaning and realize such holistic perceptions can never be known explicitly or, ii) it can simply reject or delete implicit contextual meaning from the repertoires of what then expresses itself as rational materialism.

The culture of rational materialism has an unbounded faith in explicit particulars yet this kind of exclusive focus on explicit differences always produces a world of splits, separations and fragmentations. Such a fragmented worldview was summed up succinctly by one old Australian Aboriginal man who spoke to W.E.H. Stanner as though he were speaking in verse:[2]

White man got no dreaming
Him go 'nother way
White man, him got different.
Him go road belong himself.

This old man was correct; the materialist white man has no

God and he travels a fragmented road of *heterogeneity without a context*.³ At the base of this path is the belief that explicit particulars exist independently without the need of a context. This is the Western scientific, commercial and economic worldview that splits, divides, fragments and excludes the mind and the environment and often society. This worldview translates in personal terms so that most of us work hard to achieve success through detailed, explicit and competitive methods. This is what many of us will do in our mid-twenties when we rationally organize our life into the compartments of work, lovelife, family and society. This is especially the case for those of us who are workaholics. Such people are especially prone to those rationally walled worlds that split head from heart but which can give logical proof, justification and reasoned argument for everything. However, quite often this kind of devotion to a rational materialism will create some kind of emotional crisis where life seems to suddenly lack meaning and then the individual will fall into a black hole of depression.

In contrast to the dictates of rational materialism, when the intellect serves empathy, the intellect drops the illusion that it is an infallible, objective and rational agent and becomes instead just a discerning set of features within a broader social, community and spiritual context. When the intellect is the servant of empathy it *knows it does not know explicitly* and as a consequence, embraces contextual meaning and we will then experience empathy and have compassion as the end point of our thoughts and actions. When science finally becomes empathetic it will fully encompass the contextual world of mind and Meaning.

History

Although he does not use Meaning as a focus for his argument, Owen Barfield in *Saving the Appearances*⁴ described the historical processes he sees involved in this mode of thought. Barfield bases his argument on the notion of 'participation'. He viewed 'participation' as the way in which individual and collective minds take part in, and are entangled with, the cosmic mind (of the Host). (The Zen Buddhist term 'mutual interpenetration' is perhaps close to what Barfield means by 'participation'). For Barfield, it is the changing nature of this participation that marks the differences between what he sees as three modes of thought, and the progress we make in what he calls the evolution of consciousness. Barfield's three modes of though are: *figuration, alpha-thinking and beta-thinking*. These three modes roughly equate with *desire, intellect* and *empathy*.

For Barfield, *figuration* is a subliminal pre-reflective process that transforms sense perceptions into representations, or a 'thing' in a familiar world. These processes are not equivalent to desire for they represent much more than the processes of identification. His *alpha-thinking* is concerned with the way we treat representations analytically and objectively and this mode is closely related to the intellect when it is in the service of desire. As for his *beta-thinking*, this occurs when our thinking is deliberately self-reflective and it has much in common with empathy. For Barfield, it is the changing nature of our participation in the world that marks the predominant mode of thought in society as well as the stages in the evolutionary progress of consciousness.

Barfield identifies three periods in the history of human kind that relate to our participation in the world. For example, he suggests that there was a period in the distant past that was marked by the tribal life-styles of *original participation*. He also suggests that in the future there will be a more ideal time when mutual interpenetration will be an accepted habit of society and this period he called *final participation*. The present age of science and technology he identifies with *alpha-thinking* and as a time of *non-participation*. This age of rational materialism is therefore evidenced by a progressive decline of participation from earlier periods.

Barfield argues that this decline has been accompanied by increasing degrees of abstraction. For example, he suggests that 'the gradual emergence of man from original participation amounts also to the gradual emergence of 'men' from 'man".[5] Barfield looks back on history from the twentieth century, a period in which he imaginatively describes scientific consciousness in terms of 'dashboard knowledge'.[6] Dashboard knowledge represents the knowledge available to the driver of a motorcar who looks at the dashboard but is not concerned to look under the bonnet and understand the deeper meaning of the machine.

Barfield's focus on participation certainly offers a solid foundation for a study of intellectual and conceptual change. This is an area where his argument is strongest. For example, our modern concepts of space, time and movement have meanings that were unknown in earlier times when participation was a central cultural assumption. We now commonly understand space to be a mindless, lifeless, unlimited void in which there is simply an absence of objects. In ancient times space was conceived quite differently, more like a 'mental mobile' to use Barfield's words. Space then was an extension of ourselves and we were seen as the microcosm within the larger macrocosm of space.

Similarly, the modern concept of movement is of an external object moving through a space/time continuum at a certain velocity. Within this model consciousness has no role to play since movement is assumed to be a clinical, objective operation that can be measured mathematically. Barfield reminds us that we only have to read Plato's description of the world as 'a moving image of eternity' to realize that within this ancient philosophy were embedded assumptions about our participation in the world that have now eluded most of us. For example, in ancient times metaphysics and astronomy were conceived of as one and the same.

Many of us may decide to dismiss such ancient assumptions as infantile or unsophisticated. To do this would be like the schoolboy who attends comparative religion classes and comes away with the view that 'other' religions are inferior to his. To appreciate cultural differences we must first understand and come to terms with the cultural ground on which we stand. In the absence of this self-reflective cultural knowledge there is only the bias of the uninformed. This is the case whether cultural differences exist geographically or historically. Barfield's point about participation is that the modern scientific view that constructs an independent physical world does not come from being better informed. Rather, it is a view that comes from a significant erasure of meaning. He suggests that this deletion refers to the elements of connection and participation; in terms of Meaning this is the erasure of contextual, implicit meaning.

Barfield saw the beginnings of the current scientific age as the gradual changes in thinking that occurred over a period of three thousand years, beginning with the emergence of Greek thought from the Orient and culminating finally in the rise of mechanical science four hundred years ago. From this perspective the Copernican revolution marks not a new discovery that initiated a scientific revolution but a time when the consciousness of a collective intellect finally arose from its early three thousand-year-old foundations.

Barfield's alpha-thinking represents rational materialism, a mode of thought that rejects our participation in the world and conceives of our only link to phenomena as being through the senses. Alpha-thinking is thus associated with mechanical science and speculation about a world that is separated from the observer. This is thinking that rejects our embedded participation and hence rejects the causal role of meaning, mind, life and spirit. Barfield locates some of the early semantic tendrils of this evolutionary stage within the systematic study by the ancient Greeks of astronomy. He argues that these early developments in abstract, speculative consciousness gradually transformed over several thousand years into the scientific revolution of the sixteenth and seventeenth centuries.

Today some would argue that a sense of non-participation was and is necessary so that mechanical science could be born and continue to operate in what is often called a 'parsimonious' manner. Yet non-participation directly contradicts the central epistemological premise that continued from Aristotle to Aquinas, namely our assumed participation in nature. Barfield argues that we can conclude either that this 'persistent assumption was a piece of elaborate deception' which happened to last for most of human history down to the sixteenth and seventeenth centuries or, on the other hand, we can accept that we really are part of the universe and do participate in it. If we accept participation then logically it means that our recent non-participation represents a willful blindness.

In order to balance Barfield's view on non-participation it is well to be reminded that the scientific revolution has two tendencies that are constructive as well as destructive. Thus under the tutelage of the intellect, social relations and social formations have become more open, transparent and democratic. We see evidence of this within the evolution of a modern western consciousness in what is sometimes called western liberal humanism. This is a secular religion without a God. Its ethical ideals involve the notion of merit and have provided many with the hope of finding purpose and meaning in their lives through the development of their own capacities. These humanist ideals have drawn the important secular distinction between the use of state power and religion, a combination that in the past led to persecution and pain. Secular ideals have also contributed to the important issue of stability within social formations; a stability that is based upon the rule of law, rational administration, democratic participation, universal franchise and the unifying benefits of cross-cultural diversity in which each citizen no matter their class, caste, religion or ethnicity are equal.

The social stability that flows from the ideals of western liberal humanism, together with the material wealth and physical health and well being generated by technology and science, are the evolutionary gains made by the scientific revolution. These benefits stand in contrast to those insecure social formations where tribal loyalties and or the desires of patronage play a major role in subverting or rejecting transparency and democratic processes. Thus, one of the dominant and positive outcomes for meaning making in this contemporary age has been the social balance and stability we see emanating from secular democratic institutions and nations. Barfield would argue that the downside to this period has been the dislocation of humans from nature and the cosmos brought about by a philosophy of rational materialism.

Thus because science and technology carries the infection of denial that limits our ability to see beyond appearances and disappearances, this period of great material growth has not been an entirely successful antidote to the restricted life of tribe and desire. This limitation of Reason has meant that our personal and collective desires have often found expression through the use of science and technology. In other words, science and technology have often simply given us the means for disposing of our enemies much more efficiently. On an individual level, materialistic men and women live mostly dualistic lives split between reasoned justifications on the one hand and their attempts to fulfill desires on the other. Such a life is limited because the intellect can become disoriented by a narrow technological view of the world, a view that is supported by an expert and often-prodigious use of symbols. On the other hand our state of mind is blinded by the unruly eruption of suppressed desires that are commonly expressed in terms of competitive behavior. In addition, a prodigious use of language often means a prison-house of language that can easily disorient us especially when we finally come to realize that the explicit certainties of symbols fail to solve life's problems.

Both desire and the intellect when it is serving desire inhibit our capacities to transform the mind and become self-reflective and finally empathetic. These modes of thought have a blindness that is difficult to overcome. Often the transformation from rational materialism to empathy is extremely difficult for the tertiary educated man who has become overly reliant on the explicit details of his graspable but limited known world. Yet often a crisis occurs within such a person at mid-life that heralds some kind of change of direction. A crisis often comes to the rationalist whose explicit world has been relied upon for so long it now no longer seems to provide answers to his problems. When this happens he can be left 'high and dry' in terms of understanding himself and his place in the world. With such a crisis people can often fall into a state of deep depression where the world seems to be meaningless or absurd.

The French writer and philosopher Albert Camus (1913–1960) wrote a great deal about the absurd. In his philosophical essay, *The Myth of Sisyphus* Camus undertakes to answer the only philosophical question he considers matters: 'There is but one truly serious philosophical problem and that is suicide.'[7] His essay describes how the world is unreasonable; how we live as if not knowing about the certainty of death; how rationality fails us and how science is unable to explain the world. According to Camus, when the human need for understanding meets a world that is unreasonable, the contradiction of the absurd must then be acknowledged, lived through and constantly confronted. Yet Camus' answer to his question about suicide is to say that suicide, as the philosophical answer to the absurd, should be rejected.

Camus' view of the absurd is a harsh philosophy to live by and in its recognition of the limits to the logic of reason it has some affinity with Barfield's criticism of non-participation and the current view that reason carries a virus that denies the importance of implicit meaning. However, unlike Barfield or the current approach, Camus' sense of the absurd comes from what he describes as a life that appears to be without meaning, as told in *The Myth of Sisyphus*. Yet as we are examining meaning, a life without meaning is a statement that needs examining. A life without meaning does not say how we make meaning in this life, nor does it say anything about how an absurd world is created by the way we think. Rather, Camus' absurd and unreasonable world represents an objective rational statement without qualification and, as he suggests, we just have to adjust to it.

Yet we know objective statements are essentially false. Camus' view of reason is that of an Enlightenment man who has awarded reason an infallible and unconditional authority as an end in itself. Such a view produces the objective argument that life has failed by its own terms to be reasonable and therefore it is logically absurd. However, this kind of internally consistent argument has itself failed to take account of the provisional position that the intellect holds within the ordinary mind as a secondary mode of thought and, in addition, the argument fails to consider the possibility that the world is unreasonable because we think it so. Finally, this rational materialistic argument erases the underlying nature of implicit meaning that is constantly present within the ordinary mind.

While Camus rightly rejects suicide as a philosophical response to the failure of reason, the less philosophically minded, when faced with a crisis that has been made solely by the unreasonable terms of rational materialism they may experience a sense of meaninglessness and as a consequence, may take the path of suicide. Successful suicide represents a selfish and final act of denial. What is denied in suicide is the possibility of learning and transforming the explicit details of what may appear to be an intolerable situation into something that can retain a glimmer of hope for a better and more empathetic future.

In terms of the transformation of mind from desire into empathy, depression plays a similar role as suicide but often with less severe outcomes. We become depressed when life seems meaningless, when what we have valued or held dear suddenly disappears or fails to solve a pressing problem. A sense of meaninglessness relates to a lack of explicit meaning and explicit meaning is what has made the world understandable to a society where the mainstream adheres to the dogmas of rational materialism. Thus when the world seems unreasonable or to lack meaning it is because the thinking mode of the intellect has failed us because it has worked in the service of our desires and ego. Meaninglessness and a sense of the absurd is never due to a lack of implicit meaning for this *nous* is always present and continues to exist while not depending on on any human mode of thought. The mind of implicit meaning represents the cosmic mind of the Host context and this context represents our resource and full bank account of meaningfulness, a bank account that only has to be tapped into.

Depression represents the second last stage in Elizabeth Kubler-Ross' five stages of dying. The stage after depression is acceptance. The place of depression in these five stages tells us something about the nature of depression. It tells us that depression is a stopover station on the pathway to something else. In terms of Meaning, depression is the black-hole station in which we are forced to come to terms with the bankruptcy of values and trust we had placed in analytical practices, thoughts and behavior. Thus when the body is sick or when finances fail or when we feel socially excluded we become demoralized and our ideal of a rational self (ego) suffers. It is then we have to deal with these failures through the experience of depression.

Some of us will have to experience despair and misery in order to grow, which means that depression is not a mental illness so much as a pattern of growth that needs to be worked through. A pattern of growth is a learning situation. The learning situation of depression may in some instances be helped by the short-term use of drugs. However, the limitation of anti-depressant drugs is that drugs cannot change meaning or give us a sense of meaningfulness. Rather, the learning that is necessarily involved in depression is a change that brings to light the meaningfulness of an individual's context. By this I mean the context in which the person lives. That context is discoverable whenever we learn who we truly are, when we learn to let go of the all the nonsense of the false self (the ego) and find its replacement in the implicit meaning of the Host context. This spiritual readjustment cannot be brought about by rational argument and so all prior learning patterns are quite useless when it comes to moving from an analytical 'head' process through depression to empathy.

What facilitates this transformation from *explicit to implicit* (from intellect to empathy) is a set of spiritual practices in which we continually make *implicit to implicit* exchanges. Implicit to implicit exchanges are those exchanges involved in intuition, insight and realization. They also form part of any remedial therapy that involves repetition. These *implicit to implicit* exchanges represent the essence of our holographic relationship to the divine Host and they are best facilitated by the repetitious practices undertaken in mantra meditation and/or prayer. These exchanges are not helped by reasoned argument, rather *implicit to implicit* exchanges are destroyed by such arguments.

The learning transformation of intellect into empathy is therefore facilitated by the recognition that when taken to its logical conclusions, intellectual arguments are unreasonable. In practical terms this recognition means that language, measurements or money are severely limited and will always involve the creation of the explicit world of contradictions. To move beyond the explicate order (David Bohm's terms) we have to encounter and recognize the non-explicit nature of implicit meaning. This requires a felt appreciation (not a rational argument) of empathy, unity and participation (interpenetration). The very best that the intellect is able to achieve is to employ a language that points us in the general direction of empathy and towards *implicit to implicit* exchanges. This 'very best' is always a conditional state of knowing we cannot know everything explicitly. In this state of mind the representations of language exist as nothing more than provisional signposts that point to a contextual and implicit understanding beyond the symbolic.

Finally, spiritual practice represents a learning method that can ease our way through the black hole of depression by taking us beyond the unreasonableness of the absurd to the calmer shores of empathy. This transformation is the natural progression in becoming a mature person. The learning potentials of this spiritual path may only become apparent when the hollow materialist finally admits in the depths of his depression that the light that leads out of this black hole comes from a spiritual awakening.

Chapter 9 – The Alps of Empathy

Empathy is the final mode of thought of the ordinary mind. It is buried beneath those desperate knots of desire and all the arguments, skepticism and justifications of reason. The potentials of this mode of thought have been there all the time, hidden from view but nevertheless exerting a benign influence on the way we think and see the world and act towards others. The closer empathy is to the surface of our awareness the more we allow ourselves to act compassionately as our brother's keeper. When we experience empathy the world is no longer desperate or absurd but full of love, connection and meaning.

The master narratives of religion or science do not dominate the world of empathy even though they exert some influence on the way we still think and act. We may call ourselves Christian, Buddhist, Hindu, Muslim or a rational scientist but for the person of empathy these labels are not tribal signs that separate *us* from *them*, but are the fallible route maps that provide a direction for action. Empathetic thinking and action are post-rational, post-secular, post-desire, post-nationalistic and post-ego. Yet this mode of thought does not obliterate reason, nation, ego or desire, but values them less than the implicit connections of community, compassion, love and spiritual connection.

Rather than emphasizing differences and separations, empathetic thought pays attention to what is common in all human behavior and what ties us together in communities. Specifically, empathy integrates the distinctions and differences of all narratives into larger contextual frameworks or wholes. The whole into which all narratives and all differences fit is the whole of Meaning (consciousness) of which the ordinary mind is a part. The integration of empathy is therefore brought about by the transformation involving the exchanges of the intellect (*explicit to explicit*) into the exchanges of empathy: *explicit to implicit*. *Explicit to implicit* exchanges are exchanges between context and constituent, or background and foreground. It is only within empathetic thought that the gestalt of mind (of context and constituent) can be recognized as such and applied. As a consequence of this realization, all knowledge is contextualized and every detail is seen to represent part(s) of the larger, holistic pictures of Meaning. It is well known that the context always gives meaning to any detail and it is this contextualizing process that is the hallmark of empathetic thought and action.

Empathy is commonly understood as: the *ability to imagine oneself in another's place and understand the other's feelings, desires, ideas, and actions*. While some would understand this definition to include sympathy, empathy is very different from sympathy. That difference relates to the way love is narrowed by desire and expands with empathy.

The love we experience when we desire another is constricted and narrowed by the processes of identification. These are processes that fuse together two or more objects as if they were one. This fusing process represents a narrowing of vision that is halfway between the implicitness of insight and a full conscious differentiation. Desires represent subliminal patterns of narrowed attraction that create the internal dynamics of wanting or longing. These are the common core experiences in infancy, childhood and adolescence. The love of desire is, therefore, a love that wants to cling to, and holds onto, the objects of desire. In the classical world of the Greeks, this kind of love in adults was generally understood to be a kind of madness.

In contrast, the love that always flowers in empathy is an inherent attraction that comes naturally from the underlying connections of implicit meaning. The love within empathy therefore reflects the attraction and connection of the Host: the foundation source of the mind. In other words, empathy is the ordinary mind's attempt to mirror what lies close beneath it and this is the implicit foundation of the meaning of Meaning. The force of attraction within implicit meaning means that empathy has no holding on, or clinging to any objects, and hence there are few if any conditions or qualifications in empathetic love. There is simply the fullness and recognition of interconnection that carries its own reward, which is joy. The love of empathy is perhaps close to what Socrates said about *Eros*, which he defined as a longing for wholeness or completeness. With empathy there is a taste of the wholeness of the Host, but empathy is still a thought mode of the ordinary mind so this taste of the Host's completeness remains a known but yet unrealized possibility.

From the viewpoint of Meaning, sympathy represents a pattern of identification that places us in the same situation as the other. To use an over-simplified analogy, sympathy is when we see a person at the bottom of the well unable to get out so we jump in with them. In contrast, empathy is when we get a rope and pull them out. The contrast between the passion of desire and the compassion of empathy is also the contrast between sympathy and empathy.

When empathy develops within us we start to become disentangled from our desires but also disengaged from the complex defenses of our ego. Such detachment and disengagement is unlike the scientist's idea of objective non-participation in the world, rather it involves a studied self-reflection in which the knots of our desires and ego begin to untangle in the face of this critical learning. As empathy develops our sense of personal hurt, injustice and failure also diminishes while our sense of connection and participation enlarges and becomes real. Empathy can be said to represent a wisdom that views the self not as a separate entity or a body that dies but as an eternal spiritual essence that is the central vital feature of every living organism.

When the intellect produces highly expert technical knowledge that is devoid of broader contexts, the intelligence of empathy produces wisdom that comes from integrating the differences and distinctions of technical knowledge into broader contexts of knowledge and consciousness. With the wisdom of empathy we automatically seek out and value links, similarities and isomorphic connections, whereas with rational materialism differences are emphasized and over-valued. 'Similarity' is an important meaning for the development of empathy. Similarity is a meaning that begins with differences and then reduces their individual values by locating them within broader systems and contexts.

The process involved in similarity is one that enfolds the value of individual differences and distinctions with an emphasis on their implicit connections. The enfoldment of differences and distinctions so they become aspects of similarities represents a model for the way empathy functions. Hence, empathy entails the intelligent understanding that every object and form is distinct it is also part of the unified whole of consciousness. This kind of integration can be also called compassion, which is the recognition that other people have different and legitimate interests, beliefs and destinies. This kind of understanding embodies the contradiction that things are always *distinct but unified.*

In general, empathy is a mode of thought that is open and receptive to implicit, contextual meaning and it is this kind of meaning that is always ambiguous, provisional and open to interpretation. As a consequence, empathy helps us to be aware of the possible consequences of our actions as well as the actions of others. Empathy brings together heart and head, love and intellect into inclusive realizations and intuitive connections that also have some of the qualities of extrasensory perception – a perception beyond the five senses.

Empathy represents the path of virtue. There is no other path of virtue so absolute. There is no rational or patriotic path of virtue that cannot be contradicted or qualified and there is no virtue in our desires or ego. Only the compassion of empathy stands as virtuous all the time under all conditions. When asked which is the greatest commandment, Jesus said, 'Thou shalt love the Lord thy God with all thy heart and with all thy soul and with all thy mind'; and the second, 'love thy neighbor as thyself'. (Matthew 22: 36–40) The combination of these two loves represents the absolute virtue of empathy. Empathy involves knowing the self in order to love your neighbor as your self. It is impossible to love your neighbor as yourself if you are ignorant of your self. One must begin where Jesus said to begin, by knowing and loving your Lord, which is your true self. Knowing your self always involves knowing the difference between the ordinary transient mind and your cosmic mind. This kind of wisdom resides at home within the cosmic and eternal foundation of the self, which is also the home of unconditional love. With both commandments, of loving the Lord as well as our neighbor, we become capable of knowing the subtle forces and attractions of empathy through experiencing them.

Empathy therefore grows with the growth of self-knowledge. This is the integrated wisdom of a fourfold vision; it is the wisdom of the 'heart' that comes from knowing the four levels of your mind. Empathy does not grow from expert or technical knowledge of the scriptures or from knowledge of mechanics, or science or technology. Publically performing these various kinds of technical knowledge can provide us with celebrity status but this acclaim does not make us wise or virtuous and nor does it make us more able to love our neighbor as our own true self. Only self-knowledge gained through empathy does this and only a holistic understanding gives us the force and momentum to proceed down the path of virtue.

Empathy is therefore not the result of rational knowledge and neither is it 'emotional intelligence'.[1] Having intelligence about emotions does not guarantee empathy. It may simply be the result of diplomatic training, such as the businessman receives before he visits a foreign country. In such situations this training does not obliterate the businessman's desires or self-interest; rather, it often augments it. Training to identify emotions is like studying comparative religions and this is an exercise that does not necessarily make students more tolerant or empathetic.

In addition to virtue, empathy represents the only valid and sane response to the world. 'Sane' and 'sanity' have been much used terms over the last century but their use has generally lacked any systematic context beyond the vague idea of adjusting individual needs to the norms of society, or in Erich Fromm's case, of 'adjusting society to the needs of man'.[2] As a consequence of linking human needs to some vague notion of sanity we have been served up with many pessimistic words that allegedly prove the intrinsic failures of both society and individuals.

Empathy is the sane mode of thought and its sanity resides in its multi-layered capacity to read and comprehend several levels of meaning at once. This is the ability to recognize, read and appreciate parables, allegories, metaphors and ironies. It is the ability to read and understand the subtexts of any text but in particular the four contexts of who we are. Empathy thus represents the recognition of a fourfold spiritual vision. This sane mode of thought has the capacity to appreciate that every visible form, both concrete and abstract, is underpinned by a hidden event that has given rise to such forms. The sanity of empathy is the realization that our true nature is love that connects every one of us to each other and to the rest of the universe. This is the realization that our ordinary mind is not autonomous but, rather, a unique part of the collective mind of the Host's cosmic consciousness.

A society based upon empathy does not return to a rural innocence or a pre-literate tribal paradise. Similarly, a fifty-year-old who feels the tension of a mid-life crisis cannot turn the clock back to adolescence or childhood innocence. Many may try to return to the identifications of youth through cosmetic surgery or drugs, yet these attempts amount to a failure to recognize the nature of the developmental changes that are already occurring within their ageing bodies. Empathy is therefore not a turning back, rather, it is a forward moving learning that relies a great deal upon intuition, curiosity and letting go of old habits of mind and action.

Implicit exchanges represent the basis of a spiritual life but these exchanges also help build strong communities of empathy or what sociologists call social capital. When communities are open, inclusive and pluralistic they tend to be nurturing, stable and empathetic. In such communities empathetic exchanges represent a significant social asset. This community wealth is missing from societies that are based upon coercion, power or financial rewards. Community empathy is generated by voluntary exchanges that help produce friendly and secure connections between citizens who participate freely in the community. This kind of social and democratic interaction builds a strong sense of security aligned with expectations of reciprocity and trust. The empathy values that are attached to this kind of behavior are generosity and a caring concern for the welfare of others.

Voluntary and spontaneous social interactions usually create strong connections and selfless actions that are undertaken in friendship for the welfare of others without thought of reward. They are the unplanned acts of kindness and love that come directly from our most basic implicit and connective self. These sorts of positive social actions only happen spontaneously in the present moment. In other words, they only materialize if we are not coerced, if the past is not at our back and the future not in our face. These are the acts of our true selves. The connection that comes from such interactions does not spring from the bonding of identification. Rather, this is the open connection with strangers in friendship. Spontaneous acts of kindness to strangers are also not generated by tribal law, scriptural knowledge or from logical dictates or legal rules. They come from the realization that we all are our 'brother's keeper'; that we are all neighbors in the same neighborhood.

For most of us the process of expanding self-knowledge along with empathetic capacities is slow and difficult. It can mean taking on the burden of a consciously devised strategy and perhaps a daily spiritual practice that has a focus on honest internal enquiry. It also means changing our high-energy anxieties and ego defenses into lower-energy concern for others and, in the process, helping to establish and reinforce a sense of unity in family, community and the environment. Such practices are quintessentially spiritual.

Spiritual practices may be supported by the texts of scriptures but the *implicit to implicit* exchanges of any spiritual practice are not created by language. Spiritual practices operate between the ordinary mind and our cosmic mind and such exchanges are overwhelmingly *implicit to implicit*. This caveat on language is necessary because symbolic expressions constitute explicit exchanges and these have only the status of signposts that point to another territory. As the cosmic mind of the Host context represents the first context of mind it exists prior to all symbols, texts and scriptures. In addition, the context of the Host is un-gendered. Gender is a feature of the incarnate body, the second level of mind. To believe that God is male or female, or a combination of both, is to identify the first context with the second. The Host context is the pure Spirit Supreme of implicitness. The Host is therefore without form and also without gender. It is the intelligent energy of Meaning, more subtle than a summer breeze yet the mother of all things under heaven.

Some have argued that it is easier to engage in spiritual practices if the Divine is seen to have a form and that a formless Divinity is too abstract and too difficult for most people to identify with. The argument goes that it is better for practical purposes to worship some form or image of the Divine that most people can immediately recognize. The dilemma of this strategy is that the images and forms we choose to worship have tended to become idols or cultural orthodoxies both of which reverse the natural order of Meaning. According to Owen Barfield, an idol is a representation that is not experienced as such.[3] In other words, this is an insane experience that is created by an image stripped from its contextual bearings so it no longer appears as a representation, but appears instead as a separate reality in its own right. This insanity can easily happen in the case of the traditional idolatry associated with the patriarchal 'form' of the Father.

When the idol (symbol) of the Father eclipses the formless and implicit Meaning of the Host context we reverse the natural order of Meaning. This is done when we identify the fourth level of symbols (the Father) as the foundation context. With this reversal we can become sectarian idol worshippers. To actually worship a particular form as a representation of the Divine is a subtle practice that does not rely upon the strategy of accepting without question a set of literal and orthodox scriptures. Rather, it is a difficult experiential and spiritual exercise of worshipping through the form to the formless transparency beyond. One successful example of this is the practice of some Indian worshippers who take an ordinary river stone from a creek, place it on their altar at home and then worship it as a representation of the Divine Host context which, in essence, it is.

Such an exercise is usually too abstract for most westerners; however, the dilemma of worshiping images taken from the scriptures and imbued with traditional identification patterns is that they are easily turned into non-representational idols. This is the dilemma inherent in most religious worship where we often become habituated by meaningless rituals that fail to challenge the strength of our desires. In contrast, insightful spiritual worship makes meaning through honest self-reflection, which is a practice in tune with the structure and order of Meaning. These kinds of intra-mind enquiries invoke the partnership we have with the Divine. Through this multi-layered partnership we may come to realize our true nature as divine humans.

Chapter 10 – The geology of Love

The mode of thought I call *innocent love* is not part of the ordinary mind. It is the 'no-mind' mind. In this mode of thought there is no ego, no desire, no rational thoughts, no expressions made through exchanges of signs or language. Innocent love represents our extended communal mind, an ocean full of *implicit to implicit* exchanges. This domain of innocent love acts as the bridge between the ordinary mind – made up of desires, ego, perceptions, concepts, rational and empathetic actions and expressions of one individual – and the ordinary mind of other individuals. Innocent love is also the bridge between our ordinary mind and the cosmic mind of the Host. This broad bridging 'no-mind' is an extended field made up of the isomorphic resonance of *implicit to implicit* exchanges.

Innocent love is therefore empty of all ordinary mind functions and operations; of all things and events as well as abstractions like time and space. As this mode of thought underpins and supports every function of the ordinary mind, description of it is difficult in ordinary mind terms for it exists prior to all expressions. This is the place of ordinary mind emptiness. Yet its existence tells us that everything created by the ordinary mind such as thoughts, differences, concepts, images and perceptions do not have an independent stand-alone existence. Rather, every feature and effect of the ordinary mind rests in and is dependent on the ground state of *implicit to implicit* exchanges, the conditions of innocent love.

The Heart Sutra is said to express the Buddha's most profound teaching. In the Heart Sutra the Buddha tells us that everything is 'shunyata', which is generally translated as emptiness. Emptiness that is full of heart feeling is the mode of thought I have been describing here as innocent love. With this trek through the big picture of Meaning I have refrained from using the terms and arguments of any religion or science, choosing instead to try and disentangle old and new ideas by using the vocabulary of meaning. We can say then that the emptiness of innocent love underpins all ordinary mind functions and operations, while its fullness relates to the fullness of the implicit interconnections between the ordinary mind of individuals and the Host context. In addition, implicit interconnections carry an energy charge that has 'attraction' and which; in human terms is the sensation of love. Hence, this mode of thought is full of innocent and unconditional love. It is for this reason that I describe the mode of thought as innocent love.[1]

The implicit field of innocent love extends infinitely. There is therefore nothing outside of this universal field of implicit interconnections and exchanges. William Blake prefigured the infinity of implicit meaning in his, *The Marriage of Heaven and Hell*. In that book he wrote:

> *If the doors of perception were cleansed everything would appear to man as it is, infinite.*
> *For man has closed himself up till he sees all things thro' narrow chinks of his cavern.*

Blake was using Bishop Berkeley's (1685–1753) argument that if our senses had infinite acuteness then we would perceive not more of the material world but infinity.[2] The infinite world of innocent love thus represents not what is perceived through the five senses but the extended sense of our community and cosmic mind. The existence of it gives a reason as to why and how we are social beings. The sense of the social is inherent in the unifying nature of this foundational mode of thought because at this level it makes possible the holographic (whole-to-part and part-to-whole) interconnection of individual, community and cosmos. This unifying field of thought connects each of us to the other so that it becomes possible to communicate between individuals and have the meaning of that communication understood. If, as materialists assume we had separate people with solo minds there would be no possibility of communication with other beings because our meaning making would be solo, independent and separate.

The *implicit to implicit* exchanges of innocent love reflects Rupert Sheldrake's hypothesis of formative causation. With this hypothesis Sheldrake sees the process of morphic resonance coming into operation, processes that Sheldrake describes as *like upon like*, and which can equally well be describes as *implicit to implicit* exchanges. These exchanges represent the habits of nature, habits that cut cross generations so that the same forms are continually recreated from one generation to the next. For Sheldrake these implicit exchanges signify morphogenetic fields that have an inherent memory so that current forms are developed and shaped by the intelligence of these field. Sheldrake's hypothesis gives a credible answer to the whole question of morphogenesis even though it is generally not acceptable to orthodox materialists.[3]

The hypothesis of formative causation places an emphasis on the causal intelligence of the field. This is an important feature of *implicit to implicit* exchanges for they do not represent a series of neutral transmissions. Rather these exchanges represent an infinite field of intelligence that is the agent or cause of the explicit world of things. Historically, such a field of intelligence has been spoken about as the place between heaven and earth. In Plato's *Symposium* Socrates describes this world as populated by immaterial beings that act as the envoys and interpreters between heaven and earth, so that they fly upwards to heaven with our prayers and worship and then descend with the heavenly answers and commandments.[4] Perhaps this ancient view has little currency today; however, it is worth reminding ourselves of it when coming to terms with the intermediary nature of innocent love, a mind that operate between the ordinary mind and the cosmic mind of the individual.

* * *

The *implicit to implicit* exchanges of innocent love also represent implicit knowing which, for ordinary mind understanding, is called intuition. This kind of knowing is not unconscious or repressed but is rather an active yet background feature of knowing anything and everything. These *implicit to implicit* exchanges also represent the nature of contextual meaning involving every transaction of the ordinary mind whether in the modes of desire, intellect or empathy. These three ordinary mind modes are not equal when it comes to the *implicit to implicit* contextual exchanges of intuition. The ordinary thought processes of desire and reason tend to erase or ignore the intuitive exchanges of innocent love through their narrow and focused vision. In contrast, the broader and deeper thought processes of empathy tend to acknowledge and engage directly with the implicit meaning of contexts as well as acknowledging the presence of intuition.

Because innocent love represents our community mind it is possible to communicate on this level without using signs or language, that is, verbal or written expression. When *implicit to implicit* exchanges operate between people it is commonly called extra-sensory perception (ESP). Such exchanges are called 'extra' sensory because perceptions that come to us through our five senses always involve explicit meaning. As these kinds of intuitive perceptions do not entail explicit meaning they have, under the cultural influences of Reason, tended to be seen as non-standard or 'extra'. In other words, the term 'ESP' suggests that sensory perception is all there is to perception and that a perception beyond this range is somehow 'para' normal. Yet implicit knowing is not a knowing that is added on, 'para' or 'extra' to the explicit meaning generated by the five senses in perception. Rather, this kind of intuitive knowing is always prior to the sequences of distinctions created by sensory perception. Because of this priority we should more accurately call this kind of perception *primary perception*. It is primary because it belongs to our foundation and community mind.

Robert Stone used the term 'primary perception' in his *The Secret Life of Your Cells* to describe the connection between humans and animals, humans and plants or humans and cells.[5] In contrast to ESP, *primary perception* implies a continuum of perception that runs from the Host's sight within the mechanics of our seeing through to a fourfold *implicit to implicit* vision of intuition and then to the secondary processes of sensory perception in which explicit and different forms arise. Such a continuum more accurately describes the reality of perception.

The kind of knowing that arises from intuitive exchanges differs from the kind of knowing that arises from exchanges of expressions using the five senses. The kind of knowing that arises from *implicit to implicit* exchanges is certain knowledge, in contrast to the uncertain knowledge that arises from ordinary mind expressions of desire, reason or empathy. The certain knowledge of intuition comes upon us before the reflective mind thinks, and therefore it operates pre-reflectively. It can silently come upon us when we look at a new moon on a clear night and feel awe, wonder and a unifying connection to the wider world. This is also the knowing of realizations, insights, revelations and the 'aha' reaction. Such responses can be generated when a closely held view is suddenly enlarged and we are able to distinguish the details of the trees but still perceive the contextual generality of the forest.

Implicit to implicit knowing also comes with dreams and

dreaming, and from our pre-reflective bodily consciousness, which is the context where all well executed actions are harmonized. Implicit knowing is essentially a spiritual knowing. This is the knowing expressed sometimes as faith and felt in spiritual insight and feelings of cosmic unity. Implicit interconnections can also represent those swells of tacit and inferential energy that can move us from one perspective to the next. In their deeper and quieter movements they can become the celestial floods of spiritual harmony, inspiration and love. As consciousness is a singular unity the structure of this knowing (*implicit to implicit*) is the same for everyone, hence the everyday sharing of non-verbal activities is an effortless and harmonious way of making *implicit to implicit* connections with others. These kinds of connections are the basis of community and group bonding that exists within all cultures and societies.

One example of the effects of *implicit to implicit* exchanges of innocent love is the tendency for fertile women living in close proximity to each other to synchronize their menstrual cycles. The materialistic rationale for this common phenomenon claims that this synchronizing is due to sensory cues that come from chemicals produced in the armpits of the women. This is highly unconvincing as there are all kinds of bodily variables that could accompany this kind of synchronization and none of them seem to indicate a causal and connecting link. In addition, if our reasoned approach to such questions automatically deletes implicit meaning from any consideration then there must be only one (explicit and sensory) answer.

In terms of Meaning, the cause of the synchronization of women's menstrual cycles is not to be found in the sense perception of bodily chemical reactions but is more likely to be found in the *implicit to implicit* resonance within the community mind generated by the group. This resonance has an implicit organizational potential that operates below the conscious mind of an individual and, therefore, beyond the conscious control of anyone. The organizational resonance of *implicit to implicit* exchanges has a bias towards harmony and interconnection and therefore towards synchronization. Given this permanent, persistent background influence towards connection and harmony it is little wonder that this unifying force will, in a few short months, exert an influence through the implicit group mind on the bodies of fertile women living in close proximity to each other so that their menstrual cycles are harmonized.

In *The Nature of Order, Book One*, the architect Christopher Alexander tells us that his aim is to create a scientific view of the world in which 'the idea that everything has a degree of life is well defined.'[6] Alexander, who is concerned with beauty in architecture, argues that even a wave in the ocean 'has some degree of life.' In terms of Meaning, a wave in the ocean is alive; it emits light and so has intelligence and therefore Meaning. The 'degree of life' (or the degree of meaning) we comprehend a wave to have equates to the degree to which we realize our implicit connection to it. This means that the degree to which I am able to tune into the cosmic resonance of the ocean and the wave. This implicit interconnection is always there; we just have to quieten down to feel it.

A pipe view
Scientific evidence is often gathered by methods that resemble looking through a pipe at the sky. By using such methods we can gather evidence that provides a limited view of a much larger picture. This narrowed view of mind tended to be the focus a group of scientists, led by Professor John-Dylan Haynes from the Max Planck Institute of Human Cognition and Brain Sciences. These scientists set about to measure brain activity in order to demonstrate that there is an unconscious preparation for decision-making by the conscious mind.[7] This preparation, which is indicated by prior brain activity, can take as long as seven seconds before we make a free-choice decision.

In the past this kind of response, called a 'readiness-potential', was thought to be only a fraction of a second and was often explained away by the materialistic idea that the mechanism of brain made the decision rather than the individual's mind. Since the recent study, however, it has become widely accepted that conscious decisions are unconsciously prepared. The term 'unconscious' was used by the Haynes team as a loose psychological reference for what I would call the broader no-mind state of implicit to implicit exchanges. In effect these studies confirm that the conscious decision-making processes of the ordinary mind arise out of a prior state, what these scientists called 'unconscious readiness potentials'. 'Readiness potentials' is a narrow term that refers to the infinite connecting context of *implicit to implicit* exchanges.

Innocent love has the state of ordinary mind emptiness but it is nevertheless full of implicit exchanges. The fullness of *implicit to implicit* exchanges is a plenum that represents the supporting contexts for every operation of the three modes of the ordinary mind: desire, reason and empathy. The seven seconds preparation for making a choice discovered by the Haynes team indicates the existence of a prior and supporting context to ordinary mind operations. However, the implicit field of meaning that supports and is associated with desire and reason is itself largely rejected or ignored by these two ordinary mind modes. The overall effect of such rejection means that these two thought modes tend to be resistant to learning through inner self-reflection and so may increase the delay of the readiness potential. In addition to rejecting implicit meaning, these two thought modes have the predisposition to look out towards what is thought to be the external world. As the thought processes of the ordinary mind create the external world, the capacity of desire and reason to mature much beyond their own habitual responses is reduced.

In contrast, when the ordinary mind is in the mode of empathy it is at last capable of looking to the plenum of innocent love in order to be creative with ordinary mind problems. This reflective process is sometimes called creativity and sometimes spirituality. We should note that *implicit to implicit* thought is not thinking about some-thing but a knowing before there is ordinary mind thinking. When the ordinary mind looks for answers to problems it can look in two places, i) within the conscious content of the ordinary mind or, ii) within the no-mind field of innocent love that underpins the ordinary mind. When we look for answers in conscious thought we tend to go around in circles and not find what we are looking for. When we begin to look intuitively or seek vaguely and implicitly in places that appear to be irrelevant it is always surprising how answers arise. The *implicit to implicit* exchanges of innocent love represent the fertile ground for creative thought and these exchanges operate below the level of conscious choice all the time.

Looking for solutions to problems within the no-mind field of innocent love represents various kinds of practices that have one thing in common. This is an anticipatory sense of waiting silently upon implicit meaning to transform itself into an explicit answer. Being creative often involves not doing much more than putting the question to the field of implicitness and then waiting for the answer to arise. It is a bit like fishing in the universe; you bait your hook with a question concerning a problem and then wait for a tug on the line. As the ordinary mind is part of the whole, the whole will answer usually when you least expect it and in a manner that is often not obvious. This happens when a physical event gives a significant meaning to a mental state and we then use the term 'synchronicity' to describe the coincidence of these events.

A more deliberate strategy to engage with this bridging pre-reflective mind is through focused repetitive action. Repetitive actions always increase learning ability and strengthen memory, which is an aspect of the way *implicit to implicit* exchanges function. A repetitive action establishes an *implicit to implicit* exchange for these exchanges naturally occur through repetitions. The more focused and persistent we are with any repetitive action the deeper the learning and the more proficient we become. For example, the more we practice with a musical instrument the more proficient we become at playing it. Similarly, the more we practice at the *implicit to implicit* exchanges of innocent love the more we come to realize the holographic unity of who we are. This is spiritual practice and will usually involve prayer or mantra mediation.

Cases

The implicit to implicit exchanges of innocent love are the kind of communication that often occurs between an enlightened master and a disciple. I have had a range of experiences with this kind of communication between my guru, Amma, and myself. With these exchanges nothing was spoken, written or expressed yet I was 'told', 'instructed' and 'questioned' about a range of issues related to my spiritual development. My daughter, Cleo, has also experienced this subliminal, intuitive communication. One example occurred when Cleo, my wife Amanda and I were staying at Amma's ashram in Kerala in 1997.

Cleo was then thirteen and had been reading different stories about Amma's senior disciples, many of whom had been told by Amma that they were her spiritual son or daughter. Even though she had been receiving blessings from Amma since she was nine Cleo had never been told directly that she was Amma's spiritual daughter. Desperate to be told she was Amma's daughter Cleo fell into a longing sadness, and remembering we were to leave in a few days she began crying and prayed to Amma to give her a sign as to whether she was her spiritual daughter, asking directly, 'if I am your daughter call me up for a blessing today'.

What Cleo had forgotten was that the day was set aside solely for Indians so no Westerners would be allowed to got up to the altar to receive a blessing. Both Amanda and I were oblivious of Cleo's prayer. Once Cleo had stopped crying she waiting for a time until her eyes were not so puffy and went down to the hall to join the large crowd. All day long Amma was kept busy giving hugs to the long lines of waiting people. Late in the afternoon when Cleo had forgotten about her prayer she was standing at the side of the hall with some friends when Amma motioned towards them. A nun came over to the group and said that there was no blessing for Westerners today. On returning to Amma the nun suddenly turned and came back to the group and motioned to Cleo to come. This was a surprise to everyone and was the only break from the day's protocol of no-Westerners. Cleo was duly ushered to Amma's lap where she received her blessed hug: the sign for which she had prayed.

Amma motioned to Cleo to come and sit near her and after about half an hour the mind-fog cleared enough for a spark to ignite Cleo's understanding of what Amma had done by calling her up for a blessing – more tears. This was clearly a case of spiritual communication between a Master and her spiritual daughter and in terms of Meaning it was an *implicit to implicit* exchange.

Another but different example of *implicit to implicit* exchange occurred some years later in 2005 when Cleo and I travelled to Sri Ramana Maharshi's Ashram in Tamil Nadu. We had wanted to stay at Ramana's Ashram, the Ramanasramam but had not booked ahead and were told there were no rooms available. We then went a hundred meters up the road to Seshadri Ashram where there were rooms. Seshadri was also an enlightened soul and had lived in the same location and at the same time as Ramana but had been less well-known, hence more vacant rooms in his ashram. Both Ramana and Seshadri had died many years before our visit. That first night Seshadri came to me in my dreams and offered his services to help fulfill my desires. This was a pleasant if somewhat disorienting experience, but as I was learning that travelling in India can be a pleasant but disorienting experience so this dream, which of course happened below the level of conscious deliberation, did not seem particularly strange at the time.

The next day Cleo and I set off to explore the largest Shiva temple in Southern India and then the sacred mountain of Arunachala. After we had finished our tour around the temple we set off up the mountain and somehow without any effort acquired a couple of young boys who became our guides. We wound our way up to a cave where Ramana had meditated for fifteen years. The cave was now behind a small building and on our arrival five or six people came out of the building as we went in. The cave was very clean and lit by a small candle on a central rock that rose half a meter above the floor. At the back of the cave the roof sloped down almost to the floor. On the finely polished cement floor there were cushions where we could sit and meditate. I was keen to meditate in the silence of this auspicious place and hoped that no other visitors would come and disturb us.

Cleo sat by the door, her back against the wall. I sat in front of the candle away from the light of the doorway and soon became lost in deep meditation. About half an hour into the meditation I had a vague sense that someone had come to the doorway and then gone away. I became aware after about fifty minutes of meditation that we had probably stayed long enough so we stood up and came out into the light of day. There was no one there, not even the sannyasin who looks after the cave. We could have stopped longer! I asked Cleo what her meditation was like. She said she thought she might have gone to sleep. I thought she might have had a very deep meditation.

We caught up with our guides and walked around the side of the mountain for another fifteen minutes to a compound containing a group of buildings that overlooked the temple below. I sat down to meditate again. This time it did not seem the right time or place so after inspecting the several buildings we left the compound and re-joined our waiting guides outside the compound. It had been about twenty minutes since we left the cave when suddenly a well-dressed Indian who looked about 35 years of age and appeared to be a tourist to the area came up to Cleo and immediately began talking very fast in English.

He was clearly excited and kept saying over and over, 'I cannot believe this. This has never happened to me before.'

He was not asking her for money but just repeated, 'this is incredible. This has never happened to me before'.

Then addressing Cleo directly he asked, 'Were you the girl meditating near the door'. Unsure what was she was being asked Cleo hesitated, 'Yes – Dad and I were the only two in the cave.'

By now our excited visitor had attracted a small crowd of people who were beginning to crowd around.

'Yes, this has never happened to me before'. Looking at Cleo he said solemnly, 'I have a message for you from Swamiji. Yes, I have a message from Swamiji'.

Cleo asked, 'What is the message'?

The well-dressed Indian drew himself up and looking directly at Cleo said, 'Swamiji said you should increase your meditation. This is the message from Swamiji'.

What was all the excitement about? I had been telling Cleo for years she should meditate more. This was not much of a message.

Cleo then asked, 'Who is Swamiji'?

The man said, 'Swamiji? Ramana Maharshi!'

Ramana Maharshi had been dead for fifty or so years. Here he was telling Cleo, through the intermediary of this man, to meditate more. As the import of the communication began to sink in it seemed to me both a giggle and a wonderful transcendent experience. It was a giggle because the message was so mundane, something I had been saying to her for a long time. And it was transcendent because this communication came from a realized soul who had been without a body for many years. Given Ramana's non-material state his communication to the intermediary could be only of one kind and that was *implicit to implicit*.

Skeptics would no doubt suggest that this was all a hoax and the man had simply given us this message without having received it from Ramana. My answer to such a claim is that they may be right but I doubt it. The man, who we never saw again, gained nothing by such a communication. In addition, the meaning of this communication was not only in the message, but also and more significantly, in the form of its delivery and who it came from. At the time I had no doubt at all that Ramana was speaking to us, not just to Cleo, but to the messenger as well. Since then I have not changed my mind.

If one is rationally predisposed against *implicit to implicit* exchanges of any kind, as many tertiary trained people are, then implicit communications that operate prior to the senses simply do not exist. As these exchanges do not exist, any story about them is simply a hoax: end of story! However, when one matures and passes beyond the restricted world of materialism and learns to listen to the fullness of implicit meaning beyond the explicit form, then a story of this kind is simply seen as delightful and acceptable.

A week after our encounter with Ramana Maharshi on the sacred mountain of Arunachala, Cleo and I were eating in the western canteen of Amma's Ashram that sits on the Arabian coast of Kerala in southern India. We had been at the Ashram for several days and I was feeling much in need of some protein so had ordered an egg sandwich. It was lunchtime and the two of us had found a table inside the large pavilion. The building had no side or front walls and so many of the local birds flew about picking up food scraps that were left or dropped on the floor. There were also two bronze eagles that presided over the other birds and sometimes they would steal food off the table when people were sitting having a meal.

Before our meal arrived I noticed one of the eagles sitting high up on a post that supported the building. He was looking down on the diners and must have been about fifteen meters (50 feet) away from our table. When my sandwich finally arrived I was slow to pick it up, but when I did it was halfway to my mouth when the eagle's claws struck, grabbing the sandwich with such precision that his razor sharp claws never touched my fingers. And his wings, which stretched to almost two meters, also did not touch either me or Cleo who was sitting only an arm's length way. Robbed of my sandwich in a flash! It was such a shock, and afterwards, a delight, but also I realized something about animals and telepathy.

It would have been physically impossible for the eagle to take off from his perch the moment he saw me pick up the sandwich and then fly the distance in the time it took to raise the sandwich halfway to my mouth. The eagle had fantastic timing but also something else. He knew when I was going to pick it up. He read the pre-reflective 'readiness potentials' of my mind. Rupert Sheldrake noted in his *Dogs That Know When Their Owners Are Coming Home, and other unexplained powers of animals*[8] that animals have abilities which humans rarely use in a deliberate manner. If Sheldrake is right and dogs know when their masters are coming home then dogs know this implicitly. As dogs do not express themselves symbolically they are incapable of knowing about their masters coming home explicitly, symbolically or rationally.

Before I consciously decided to pick up my sandwich the eagle intuitively knew what I was going to do. He knew this implicitly and knowing implicitly is a superior, and fast way of knowing. *Implicit to implicit* exchanges are normal for humans as well as for dogs, and eagles, because implicit meaning is the unmediated base of all ordinary mind meaning-making. Without this common base there could be no exchanges of meaning of any kind. And this is a base that we share with each other and with all creatures.

Perhaps the most common experience of innocent love is those repetitive exchanges we all have experienced between mother and child. At birth our mind is largely filled with implicit feelings, a vast intuitive field connecting us to our mother and the Host context. This tacit field of comprehension is the foundation for a set of developmental processes that gradually unfolds and transforms, and then becomes a stable set of features we call character. The first six months in an infant's life is thus a significant region of influence that affects later growth and development. This region of influence represents the implicit field of mother and child and Host. This field is not a 'blank slate' but, rather, it represents implicit exchanges full of the primary potentials of a yet to be developed character. Although separate from each other in space, both mother and child form a symbiotic whole; a single unified field of implicit coherence.

With his psychoanalytic approach to child development, Erik Erikson called this first phase a time when the infant develops a sense of trust or mistrust. In the cognitive theory of Jean Piaget the first two years represent the sensory motor phase of child development.[9] In terms of Meaning the first six months in an infant's life is dominated by the *implicit to implicit* structure of feelings and intuition. This structure has a natural organizational bias in favor of love, connection and dependency. Trust is created when this natural bias for love is supported. Mistrust develops when this implicit structure is unsupported. These tendencies for trust and mistrust occur because they are natural responses to the implicit interconnecting field of mother and child.

The infant's capacity to learn during this early period results from exchanges of meaning that occurs within the innocent love of this field. These exchanges are overwhelmingly implicit but over the first six months there also will be a growing number of identifications and recognitions associated with sensory motor activity such as vocal intonations, body movements and what child psychiatrists call 'mental cueing'.

The organization of this field of mother and child will therefore gradually change over time and these developments are tied to the child's increased capacity for greater levels of identification, and then of differentiation and specialization. These developmental processes create an ever-changing balance between the child's inherent tendency for connection and love and its tendency towards autonomy associated with greater levels of specialization and differentiation. A child's physical mastery over itself and its environment therefore rests firmly on this inherent field of implicit exchange which the child shares with its mother.

In the first six months there are massive implicit exchanges of meaning occurring in this field. These exchanges will largely flow from the implicit meaning of the mother, and the immediate parental environment (usually involving other parental figures), through the pre-reflective community mind to register as implicit understanding in the child. Some portion (depending upon the family structure) of these exchanges can be negative. For example, the predispositions and desires of the mother will usually be made up of patterns of identification. In addition, the mother's attitudes at times can be associated with the agitation that arises from unfulfilled desire or an over-active intellect. These attitudes and responses, which inherently arise from implicit meaning, will be subliminally (implicitly) transferred across this field to the infant to affect its understanding of the world. In this manner an infant can take on the subliminal predispositions and attitudes of its parents without any conscious thought.

Out of the initial structure of feeling there grows, though the seeds of sensory identification, the capacity for the child to locate itself as distinct from its mother and physically autonomous. At around six months of age the normal infant can differentiate sufficiently so as to assertively create and recognize the boundaries of its own body image in a mirror and recognize this as distinct from its mother's image. When this level of identification and differentiation is reached, the implicit unity of the mother and child field is not broken; rather this is simply the beginning of a more complex developmental stage. Between some mothers and children this implicit field of love is never broken and continues on permanently as a background resonance throughout life.

In Donald Winnicott's view the learning objective of the child is a search for reality, not an attempt to escape from it.[10] From the viewpoint of Meaning, this is correct. The child is in search of the reality that learning presents, that is, of the joy of unfolding all the implications of its growth. This discovery activity is associated with everything that he or she experiences. The implicit field of mother and child will thus gradually transform over the years and, with that change, the child's capacity to use explicit meaning increases and becomes more specialized in a range of areas. Gradually the child will employ more and more complex systems of the ordinary mind such as a language and a repertoire of behavior that can convey a diverse range of meanings. However, children differ widely in their capacity to learn and each child will set its own pace through its ability to handle and comprehend wider areas and more complex, explicit differentiation. This means that some children will want to be kept immersed in the implicit energy field of mother and child for longer periods than others.

This unity of the mother and child can be seen as an echo of the cosmic unity we all experience even though many of us will be unaware of it. The role of the mother in this resonant field is like that of a surrogate to the cosmic Host. The mother is the infant's host. She provides the resting and holding context in which the infant can grow and develop. This context of support is a self-similar replication of the universal Host that holds all of us within a cosmic embrace in order for us to develop spiritually.

The cosmic Host is thus the mother of us all. At a local level, the mother's love and support provides the child with continuity for the many maturation and environmental changes the child will experience. The 'mother unity' is the child's first lived experience of wholeness, a wholeness that can only ever be created through the intuitive exchanges of *implicit to implicit* meaning. If the ordinary mind of empathy represents a glimpse of wholeness then innocent love is the spiritual path that leads to wholeness. And we are supported implicitly along that path of wholeness by the implicitness of the cosmic Host.

Chapter 11 – The Big Picture

The difference between the big picture and the small picture is size. The big picture includes everything: the physical world as well as mind, meaning and consciousness. The small picture excludes mind, meaning and consciousness. The perspective of rational materialism creates the small picture while the perspective of Meaning and empathy creates the big picture. The big picture of Meaning always includes the small picture but in the process modifies rational materialism so that the intellect works in the service of empathy. A second difference is that the big picture is holistic while the small picture is always a partial or sequential view of things. The small picture can therefore never include the big picture. The partial view in science is maintained by frequent calls to the virtues of parsimony associated with the principle of 'Occam's Razor'.

For the big picture the central issue is love: how much and how many things can we love. The central issue for the small picture is how to maintain an internal logic and defend the narrow view against the possible backsliding of colleagues who become interested in a world beyond the measurable. As Kathleen Raine has written, 'Orthodoxy, in our world, means scientific orthodoxy, and although the conclusions of science in some particular areas may be open to question, the premises of the materialist orthodoxy are not.'[1]

Yet the unscientific is always clearly defined by the orthodox scientist and represents those activities that are beyond the sight lines of the small picture. For example, as Kathleen Raine goes on to argue, 'it is 'unscientific' to attribute to 'nature' any purposes, or qualities . . . or meaning of whatever kind.'² This is an easy conclusion to reach because the small picture of materialism has already rejected meaning as being part of the picture. The universe is therefore conceived by the adherents of the small picture as dead, insentient, lifeless, while human subjectivity is seen as isolated and separate; a mere stimulus response by-product of the physical body. The question of reality: of what is 'real', is thus answered by materialists as those quantities that can be measured. It follows quite logically from this limited view that what represents unreality is, that which cannot be measured, such as Meaning or consciousness. One could almost fall in love with this kind of certainty!

In contrast, reality for the big picture is the infinite interconnected nature of meaning and Meaning. These states are inseparable from each other and from the condition that I call the intelligent energy of relationships: life. Relationships construct matter as well as the ordinary mind that in turn has emanated from the cosmic mind. Summarizing Blake's total vision of reality, Kathleen Raine wrote, 'Everything that lives is holy – not holy because we choose to think it so, but intrinsically so.'³ The holy is alive but it cannot be measured, but neither can it be denied by an empathetic and integrated mind. Similarly, *To see a World in a Grain of Sand/And a Heaven in a Wild Flower* is to make meaning that is integrated and holistic that in turn gives us a fourfold vision, which also cannot be denied by the integrated sightlines of the big picture.

The vocabulary of connection and integration and the qualities of love and empathy thus give us the big picture while the small picture comes from the binary logic of materialism: two kinds of meaning and two modes of thought and perception. There is nothing wrong with a limited picture of the world if it can be recognized as limited and provisional but this is hardly ever the case. Unfortunately the small picture of materialism involves the overwhelming tendency to assume itself to be a big picture that is complete and certain. The certainty of this false completeness has withered life within nature and mortified the entire universe for us; these rational processes have erased meaning from our ordinary collective mind and reduced the value we place on community. Meaning in general is diminished when the indivisible mind is divided. This is the schizophrenic tendency of the small picture when it divides the unity of inner and outer worlds.

The unity of the universe, of inner and outer is an integrated wholeness of the One, which is the ancient kingdom of *unus mundus*. This unity of interconnection represents the big picture reality of our lives and it is this reality of a singular consciousness that we need to heed once again. The reality of the One consciousness tells us that the outer world of material things is nothing more than features of the inner world of perception: appearances – specifically, that the extensions and matter of the physical world are created by the codes and relationships of Meaning. In this culture, the differential relationships of meaning are isolated and then prized so much by logical reason that the mind from which they were given birth is ignored. Such differences then appear to stand apart and alone as objective physical reality.

Kathleen Raine wrote, 'For Blake, as for Berkeley, Swedenborg, and the ancients, time and space are mental concepts.'[4] By this she meant that time and space are within the mind and not the other way around. This is the big picture view of space and time. The small picture view is that space and time are physical and independent of an observing solo subjective mind. Here again is the cut that separates inner from the outer, for space and time are supposed to be features of the outer and objective world and the observing solo mind is supposed to be the world of inner subjectivity. Yet how is objective space different from perceptual space? There is no material and rational answer to this question because it is impossible to find such differences. Hence there are no difference between perceptual space and objective space because they are the same. The whole of space is entirely within the mind of Divine humanity, which is the composite of the ordinary mind and the cosmic mind. Space arises through our perceptual processes and it is given a non-subjective presence by the universal relationships of Meaning. This makes space both cosmic and beyond the individual mind yet part of each individual's ordinary perceptual mind. Space is therefore a feature of Meaning, and it is constituted by the cosmic mind as well as the ordinary mind of individuals working in concert. The integration of the cosmic with the ordinary results in the state of Divine humanity, a state in which each one of us is an ordinary human and also holy Divine.

For Christopher Alexander a building or a town is only alive to the extent that it is governed by what he calls 'the quality without a name'. Alexander believes that this quality is the 'root criterion of life and spirit in a man, a town, a building, or a wilderness.'[5] How to define this quality without a name? Alexander attempts with a series of terms: 'alive', 'whole', 'comfortable', 'free', 'exact', 'egoless', and finally 'eternal'. Each term he examines and then abandons because each name fails to adequately capture the quality.

In this trek through the big picture I have written about the states, codes, structure and laws of Meaning but I am unable to adequately name the implicit quality of Meaning. This is a quality implied by such words as *meaning, mind, life, spirit, joy and love* but it is a quality that is not captured by any name or list of names. Trying to define the quality of Meaning is like trying to define the quality that emanates from a relationship. We can say that a relationship is a connection of some kind, but what is that quality of connection and what gives it its connect-ability? In addition, we can speak about space as having three extended dimensions, and once we have accounted for these by reference to non-symmetrical and asymmetrical relationships of perception we are left with the implicit background of space. What is this quality? I could say that space without dimensions has the quality or potential of implicitness, but such words seem inadequate.

Scientists ask important questions about the composition of matter, for example the composition of elementary particles like photons that exhibit the characteristics of waves as well as particles. But a more important and prior question has always been: what is the basic software language of the mind. Like a computer the mind needs a basic software language through which and by which it can operate. Unlike a computer the basic software language of the mind does not begin with computation and symbols, (the fourth level of mind) but with the codes, structures, relation and principles of Meaning.

Unlike a computer the basic software language of the mind is alive, luminous and creative: it represents the sight within the bodily processes of seeing? Materialists will say that visible light (photons) is responsible for our sense of sight. This is entirely false. Visible light is actually invisible and in any case turning on a light can never bring back life to a dead body. Life is the quality of the codes, structures, relation and principles of Meaning; it is a quality that creates sight, insight, recognition, realization and understanding. These are the prior conditions that must be in evidence before any scientific experiment or measurement can take place. Yet these prior, Divinely given conditions have been consistently ignored or erased from the scientific view of the universe.

I could go on to ask: what is the quality inherent in love and attraction? This is another quality of the basic software of the mind, but it a quality we nevertheless often try to name. We call it 'I am'. *'I am that I am'* is what God said to Moses when asked for His name (Exodus 3: 14). If we accept this translation then the quality of *I am-ness* not only represents me but this vocabulary also signifies that this essence is God. Thus this first person singular present indicative 'am' – that is, 'me' – represents a nameless quality that cannot be pierced by weapons, or burnt by fire, or wet by water or dried by the wind.[6] Each of these conditions will affect my body, and only by that indirect route do they affect me. In general, my body is affected by pleasurable sensations, like having my hair brushed or by painful sensations, like being burnt. These bodily pains or pleasures usually carry with them some kind of meaning related to the context in which they occur, and which then can affect 'me'. What then can affect me directly?

The quality, *I am* is directly affected by meaning, by what others, and I say, do and think, by positive meanings and by negative meanings. Thoughts and expressions create relationships and it is these items that represent the special conditions under which meaning is made and remade. I am directly affected by the meanings of these because the field of relationships that constitutes the quality of *I am* is a meaning-scape – not unlike a landscape. The subject of *I am* can therefore be given the predicate: 'meaning' as in: 'I am meaning'. The meaning of *I am*, like true love in the Shakespearian sonnet (116) is an ever-fixed mark.[7] Even though it is the quality without a name I have called it the mystery of the meaning of Meaning.

To be confident of who I am is not the same as being confident about the meanings I make or those that are made by others. A spiritual confidence comes with knowing who I am while arrogance arises from placing too much confidence in what I or others say and think. There is therefore, an important distinction here that is often overlooked. This is the distinction made by Sonnet 116 between true love and Time's fool that alters within brief hours or weeks.

The distinction is this: the meanings that we make by thinking and expressing ourselves are always relative. They are Time's fool; they are always open to change, alteration and impediment. There are no exceptions to this rule, even for the laws of physics or the texts of the sacred scriptures. In contrast, however, the potential for making meaning admits to none of these impediments. This quintessence is beyond time's sickle. This is the meaning of Meaning, which is an ever-fixed mark. This timeless, nameless, infinite potential to make meaning is the essence of who *I am*. It also represents the life within the universe as well as the potential for the sight within the perceptual processes of my seeing. Confidence in this potential can give me a spiritual life full of love. This life filled with love exists because the potential to make relative meanings has itself the character of unqualified love. This is an infinite unnameable potential to love and be loved without imposing conditions.

In other words, unconditional love gives us the potential for making relative meanings. This essence of unconditional love can be realized when we stop everything, all thought and action, and feel the implicit union with the whole. Sonnet 116 could have been written with Meaning in mind for the same distinction between the relative and the absolute sits equally well with love as it does for Meaning. My confidence in who I am rests on the intuition that my essence is unconditional love and that this essence is also God, '*who is our home*'. As William Wordsworth (1770–1850) wrote in his *Ode: Intimations of Immortality*:

> *Our birth is but a sleep and a forgetting:*
> *The soul that rises with us, our life's Star,*
> *Hath had elsewhere its setting,*
> *And cometh from afar:*
> *Not in entire forgetfulness*
> *But trailing clouds of glory do we come*
> *From God who is our home.*

This quintessence of Meaning is thus eternal and hence unable to die because it is beyond Time's sickle. Ancient Greek as well as Indian Vedic philosophy also affirm immortality.

Immortality is the central belief at the heart of the Hellenic and the Hindu big picture world and has been the central principle of reflective humanity for the last three thousand years. Here for example is one of the oldest recorded prayers in existence and from the Brihadaranyaka Upanishads:[8]

> *OM – Lead me from the unreal to the real, from darkness to light, from death to immortality.*

Traditionally, poets and philosophers have spoken of immortality as the soul's immortality and a supreme example of this comes from the English poet, Shelley's *Adonais*, that great celebration of Keats. When referring to *Adonais*, Kathleen Raine gives us a sense of the immortal by reversing our usual understanding of dying when she says, 'the generating soul 'dies' from eternity into the time world, to resume its native immortality at death and it is this doctrine, not some fancy of his own that Shelley affirms in those burning lines familiar to us all:'[9]

> *The One remains, the many change and pass;*
> *Heaven's light for ever shines. Earth's shadows fly;*
> *Life, like a dome of many-coloured glass,*
> *Stains the white radiance of Eternity*

Dear reader, you may think me a fool to have confidence in love and immortality, or to see the whole of creation through Plato's words, as 'moving images of eternity'. If it can be shown that I am wrong and we are not divine human beings who seek after the peace of eternity then I have made no meaning with this text, which has never been written.

Postscript

After writing the manuscript of this book I took a trip to India with my nephew, Richard. I had never spent much time with Richard so we decided to go to Delhi and then on to Rishikesh without any plan to see how we would get along and what the Gods could offer us. My guru, the Kerala saint Amma had given me Rishikesh as a spiritual name so I was interested to see what if any resonance may arise from our visit to this place. However, on arriving we had decided on the trek up to Gaumouk, the source of the holy Ganga River. In Hinduism the river is worshipped as the goddess Ganga.

On this adventure we met two young German women, Anna and Petra who were fellow travellers and easy to be with in a laid-back sort of way. The trip up to Gaumouk appears in hindsight to be a reflection of the experience of writing this book and this is why I have included this piece as a postscript.

* * *

In Gaumouk, at the source of the sacred Ganga it happened. I fell to my knees amongst the rocks overcome with something more than emotion. I had not expected this reaction, but there it was, an overwhelming sense of a divine silence more vibrant than any words. There was no special light or vision just a weakness in the legs along with a strong sense of another world pulling me towards it. Richard, a trained paramedic, came up from behind and asked if I was okay. He thought I might be exhausted from the trek and the altitude as it was close to four thousand meters and the air much thinner than normal. Wiping tears from my eyes I told him I was alright and as he could see I was not having a heart attack he seemed content with his quick medical diagnosis: odd but normal behavior for this particular uncle.

I had come to Gaumouk thinking I was going to die. That thought was both liberating and fearful and it had both physical as well as mental elements. The physical basis of this thought came from our terrifying jeep ride up from Rishikesh to Gangotri, the town from which we began our trek. This was a road trip that follows along cliff faces formed over thousands of years by the swirling waters of the Ganga hundreds of meters below.

For this visitor, driving on Indian roads always involves taking many short breaths. However, after the first couple of days I begin to comprehend some of the road rules, like give-way to vehicles that are bigger than you. This was the kind of driving we experienced on the seven-hour taxi ride from Delhi to Rishikesh. But the road trip up to Gangotri was something entirely different. In literally hundreds of places much of the road had slipped into the ravine, washed away by the river recently swollen by monsoon rains. At one stage we drove the jeep through a small village slowly slipping into the Ganga. It was here we drove through what used to be a house, half of which had already ended up in the river. We continued on, passing many oncoming trucks on half a road where the edge fell away almost perpendicular into the ravine, but as we were driving on the hill side of the road and not out on the edge I began to feel perhaps we would make it after all.

Then we crossed the river so we were now on the outer edge of a narrow windy road that looked like it had been hacked out of the cliff face. The road had no safety rails and many blind corners which we took far too fast for my liking as I was now sitting on the outside of the vehicle looking straight down to boiling

Trekking the Big Picture

rapids at least two hundred meters below. On one very tight corner I unbuckled my seat belt with the thought of jumping out if we went over the edge. I then realized this strategy was idiotic as I would have been killed in any case with or without my seat belt. After far too many kilometers of this kind of eye-bulging driving I began to accept my fate and gave myself up to the distinct possibility of death by car crash.

This road experience was the visceral part of the sense that I was going to die that I had brought to Gaumouk. The other element was mental and came from my long held desire to bundle up all my fears and leave the package under a rock at Gaumouk. I prayed for this to happen for several days before we arrived at the source of the Ganga for it seemed to me that this special spiritual place was the right spot to leave my fears. I knew that if I lost my fears I would also loose my ego for the ego is a set of identification patterns held in place by fear. To loose one's ego is the same as dying, hence the idea of dying heightens our fear.

Together the jeep drive and the prayer for relief from fear produced a fearful yet liberating sense of expectation about Gaumouk. What would happen? This internal question was then mediated to some extent by the unplanned social context that Richard and I found our selves in on the trek up from Gangotri to Gaumouk. Leaving Gangotri on a sunny morning we had been walking for several hours when we came upon a tent that sold chai and chapattis to the passing pilgrims. We took off our packs and rested and revived ourselves with a drink and then began to speak to our fellow pilgrims who were there. Thirty minutes later when we left we walked out of this little oasis as a group of five: Anna, Petra, Nellie, Richard and myself.

Anna and Petra were from Germany and Nellie from Sweden. As we slowly walked and talked our way up the track we began to uncover common connections and in this process a wealth of social capital and friendship was unearthed that has enriched our lives ever since. As we walked I began to feel blessed that

Richard and I should have the company of three Sophias on this pilgrimage to the source of the sacred goddess Ganga. I felt their company like the happen-stance of this trek, had came from the intervention of the Himalayas gods who seemed to have a bittersweet sense of humor. Why bittersweet? Well everything that happened on this trek seemed to have both a difficult and delightful side. While the three young women were delightful the trek itself had many difficulties.

In the late afternoon we arrived at Bhojbasa, a desolate campsite in the rock-strewn valley above the tree line. On the southern side of the valley rose the six thousand five hundred meter snowy peak of a perfectly shaped mountain called Shivling. Ahead were the several Bhagirathi Peaks that also rose to six and half thousand meters and wore cloud hats and scarves. These Himalayan Mountains were stunning beautiful in contrast to the little settlement of Bhojbasa. That night the five of us slept in beds in a tent provided by the Uttarakhand Forestry Department but with the temperature dropping to many degrees below zero it was one of the coldest and most uncomfortable nights I can ever remember. In the early morning we sat around Richard's little stove drinking his hot tea and eating his dried food. For many years Richard was a park guide in Tasmania and so never went on any trek without adequate provisions.

He fed the five of us and it was just as well because the Forestry Department's food left a lot to be desired. We started off late for Gaumouk and finally reached it around lunchtime. As we came closer to the glacier where it transformed into the Ganga there was an increased sense of excitement. I was within a few hundred meters of the source of the Ganga when suddenly I fell to my knees. This was an unexpected and somewhat unwelcome turn of events as I generally try an avoid making a spectacle of myself. However, after succumbing to the overwhelming joy that Gaumouk seemed to generate I continued on with the others to the edge of the glacier from which the now new waters of the Ganga arose. Here at last was the very source of this most sacred of rivers.

We sat on rocks and had lunch in the sun almost under the overhanging ice cliff of the glacier. No one else was there. It was so peaceful and quiet. I took my boots and trousers off and bathed in the icy waters of the Ganga for the river is supposed to wash way sins and at this spot there was no pollution. Warming myself after the freeze of the water I had a sense of completion at this place of peace and stillness. I think the peace affected all of us in the way that deep meditation can have an effect, through a kind of vibrant silence that deepens the breadth and brings peace to the heart.

Lying back in the warm sun with my eyes closed I slowly realized that every so often rocks were falling from the overhanging ice face and on further inspection I saw that we were sitting in a spot where there were many shards of broken rock on the ground. Among the rocks there were also blocks of ice slowly melting. The realization dawned on me that the large rock directly above us on the edge of the ice cliff could at any moment join our lunch party. So we packed up and moved away from this place of peace and danger.

As the others left the glacier I sat down, out of danger from falling rocks, to say a prayer of thanks for the experience of Gaumouk. I began by saying the sacred Sanskrit syllable OM three times, out loud. This is a part of my normal meditation practice, yet here the sounds were different. They seemed to happen by themselves in an infinite universe that was here but not here, a universe in which I was not a separate identity but a participant. In this moment I felt a unity of being; my being with the being of all beings. This connection happened in a dimension that was not physically here but quintessentially mentally here. It was as if the mental background of observing the physical environment had become an infinite foreground that was in no way related to a private observation. In spite of the fact that I meditate daily this experience of unity was a shock to my mind, a mind that is generally so busily attuned to the material domain of everyday life. To be part of the unity of the universe is a revelation, an epiphany; it is the realization of an essential truth that cannot be denied or held in abeyance.

In a state of mindless serenity I caught up to the others who had stopped to have a blessing from a sadhu who lived for most of the year in a small rock enclosure about a kilometer from the ice shelf of Gaumouk. While Petra was receiving a blessing from the sadhu the others stood around in silence. I sat close by on a smooth granite rock, content not to have a blessing. Then, quite suddenly, I was being pulled skyward by an attraction that felt like the force of a huge magnet. It was not the pull of someone tugging at my sleeve; it was a force of attraction that I had never felt before and it was pulling not my body but my being. Thinking about it afterwards, I realized this was a sublime force that conveyed a sense of unconditional and fulfilled love.

The goddess Ganga traditionally represents the vehicle of ascent from earth to heaven and that is exactly what I was experiencing – the beginning of an ascent to heaven. To actually experiencing the goddess' heavenly power and potency was so astonishing and bewildering that I resisted – fool that I was. The overwhelming thought that kept coming into my head over and over was: 'I can't go, I can't die now. I have duties and responsibilities to attend to'. This extraordinary experience lasted no more than thirty seconds to a minute and left me feeling disoriented and groggy. It took several kilometers of walking to regain my normal sense of where I was.

This episode reminded me of Adela Quested's strange experience in the caves in E.M. Forster's novel, *A Passage to India*. Forster never explains what happened to Adela in the caves so the reader is left with an unsolved mystery. Forster comes close, not to an explanation but a justification when he refers to the unknown thus: 'how can it be expressed in anything but itself'?[1]

He is right of course. As soon as we write or speak about a spiritual or mysterious event they falls under the excluding rules of grammar and syntax and so becomes something quite reduced and different.

For several weeks afterwards, when thinking about this out-of-this-world episode, I felt I had failed the test. I had gone to Gaumouk praying to be rid of my fears, which in effect meant that my ego would die. I would die because the ego always constructs itself as me. Yet when I was presented with the opportunity to die I did not take it, rather I reverted to the tired old shibboleth of duty and responsibility. These excuses are held in place by a fear of letting go, of completely letting go and giving myself fully to the unknown attraction of eternal and heavenly love.

Now as I write these words some months later I have accepted my Gaumouk failure to let go. I do not see this lack of courage as a negative to be registered against my soul in some karmic library, rather I think it represents a doorway that I did not go through but which nevertheless is now always a real and close enticement. This failure to die has given me a sense of liberation. It has enriched my life and changed my view of death. I now know that when I do finally drop the form I will be propelled through that heavenly doorway willingly.

Had there been something about Rishikesh that I found familiar or with which I could identify? I am not sure. Before we left Rishikesh for Gaumouk both Richard and I went down to the river and placed small flower boats on the Ganga at the six of clock Arati ritual and watched them float away in the twilight. In my little boat I placed all my fears and desires that I was hoping to lose. I think I lost some on the trek but the ego continues to hide amongst the foliage of my mind. As for my spiritual name of Rishikesh, the place itself did not seem so special; rather it was special in what it led to. It led me to the heavenly doorway of my true Self.

Endnotes

Chapter 1

1 This was the Gyuto Monks of Tibet Program from the 3rd September to the 15th September, 2010, Mawson Place, Hobart, Australia.
2 David Bohm, *Wholeness and the Implicate Order*, (London: Ark, 1983.)
3 Materialism is usually understood in philosophy as the doctrine that whatever exists is either matter or entirely dependent on matter for existence. The related term 'realism' denotes the doctrine that physical objects exist independently from being perceived. These views of the world are often contrasted to idealism – the doctrine, which maintains that the real is of the nature of thought. While the history of the Positivists is well known the intellectual frame out of which they grew is less well appreciated. This frame was established by the advent of a modern and a highly developed technology and a science based upon a rational scientific method. These two influences produced an intellectual framework that was buttressed by the conventions of viewing the world through the prism of a series of language crimes. These language crimes were taken up and celebrated by the Positivists to the degree that they became the basis for the religion of Positivism, the founder of which was Count Henri de Saint-Simon (1760–1825). The philosopher John Gray suggests that the Positivists did not aim to merely revolutionize society (they were critical of capitalism), their aim was to found a new religion. John Gray, *Al Qaeda and what it Means to be Modern*, (London: Faber and Faber, 2007) 30. Saint-Simon envisaged a religious assembly of 'the twenty-one elect of humanity' which were to be called the Council of Newton. This religious cult soon acquired all the paraphernalia of a church – hymns, alters, priests in their vestments and its own calendar. Gray says that the transformation of Positivism into a religion, after Saint-Simon's death, was completed by Auguste Comte (1798–1857) who had an almost unlimited faith in

the power of social engineering. Over the last three hundred years the religion of Positivism came into existence and then vanished. Today the influences of Positivism are not religious but cultural. These influences continue 'to blow' as Hans Kung says: Hans Kung, *The Beginning of All Things*, Translated John Bowden, (Grand Rapids, Michigan: William B. Eerdmans Publishing Co., 2007), p 96.

4   Kathleen Raine, *Blake and Tradition*, Vol 2, (New York: Princeton University Press, 1968), p 189.

5   Kathleen Raine, *The Underlying Order and other essays*, Edited and Intro., Brian Keeble, (London: the Temenos Academy, 2008), p 107.

6   Henri Bergson, *Creative Evolution*, Trans. Arthur Mitchell, (Lantham: MD: UPA, 1983).

7   John Carroll, *The Existential Jesus*, (Melbourne: Scribe, 2007), p 25.

8   HRH, The Prince of Wales, Tony Juniper & Ian Skelly, *Harmony: a new way of looking at our world*, (London: Blue Door, 2010), p 119.

9   Swami Vivekananda, *Letters of Swami Vivekananda*, (Calcutta: Advita Ashram, 1998), pp 68–71.

10 Mata Amritanandamayi Devi, wikipedia.org/wiki/Mata_Amritanandamayi

11 Kathleen Raine, (2008) op cit, pp 41, 42.

Chapter 2

1   Quoted in: C.G. Jung, *Synchronicity: An Acausal Connecting Principle*, Trans. R.F.C. Hull, (Princeton University Press, 1973) p 70.

2   Bohm, David & Hiley, B.J. *The Undivided Universe*, (London: Routledge,1995).

3   Henry Strapp, 'S-Matrix Interpretation of Quantum Theory', *Phys Rev D3*, (March 1971) pp 1303–1320.

4   Dean Radin, *The Conscious Universe: The Scientific Truth of Psychic Phenomena*, (San Francisco: Harper Edge, 1997), p 270.

5   See for example the recent online article, 18th April, 2007 'Physicists bid farewell to reality?' in: News@Nature.com

6   I cannot say if Meaning represents what scientists have been calling 'ether'. The existence of ether in the form of ether drift and ether wind was a question asked in the 1887 ether-drift experiment of Albert Michelson and Edward Morley. After what was reported to be the neg- ative results of these experiments the idea of 'empty space' was fully embraced by mainstream science. Yet many scientists continue to dis- agree with the idea of empty space. James DeMeo had this to say about the mainstream scientific view, 'I submit, these [*the propositions that space is empty and immobile, and the universe is dead*] are unproven, and even *disproven* assertions, challenged in large measure by Dayton Miller's exceptional work on the ether drift'. Dayton Miller's Ether-Drift Experiments: A Fresh Look: http://www.orgonelab.org/energyinspace.htm This is a useful website in which DeMeo has brought together many of the original papers and experiments on ether and ether-drift. However, the question of the existence of ether and whether space is empty are two distinct questions. I leave the question of ether to others, however, regarding the question of whether space is empty and the universe dead, I argue in this work that space is full of the relationships of Meaning, which are alive.

7   The evolution of consciousness is more fully discussed in Andrew Lohrey *Speaking of the Numinous: the meaning of meaning*, (Falmouth: Rishi, 2010).

8   James Lovelock's idea of Gaia (James Lovelock, *The Revenge of Gaia: Why the Earth is Fighting Back – and How We Can Still Save Humanity*, (Melbourne: Allen Lane, 2006)) proposes that the planet Earth is a living system: Gaia. This system, which includes the biosphere, 'has kept our planet fit for life for over three billion years.' Lovelock calls this system physiological because it has the 'unconscious goal of regulating the climate and the chemistry at a comfortable state for life.' These are strange words to describe a physiological system. An 'unconscious goal' is a phrase which relates more accurately to mind, intelligence and Meaning. I would argue that the vast system of Gaia involves not only an Earth-wide self-regulating system but must also embrace a connecting inter-galactic regulating system. Such a universe-wide system would then have the goal to regulate all conditions, organic and inorganic so that the Earth's conditions are fit for life forms. In addition, the use of the term, 'self-regulation' suggests much more than the involvement of some physiological mechanism. It implies a system of Meaning that is cosmic.

9   See for example, Morphogenic Fields, Rupert Sheldrake, *The Rebirth of*

Nature: New Science and the Revival of Animism, (London: Rider, 1990), p 87.

10 Ibid. p 89.

Chapter 3

1 Northrop Frye describes Beulah like this: 'Beulah for Blake is the earthly paradise, the state of innocence, the peaceable kingdom and married land of Isaiah 11:6 and 62:4. Beulah in Blake is much the same as the holiday world of the imagination that I identified earlier with literature and the other arts, where there is entertainment without argument.' http://northropfrye-thedoublevision.blogspot.com/2009/02/chapter-two-double-vision-of-nature.html

2 For an example of this view see, D. J. Avery, 'Women and Wiliam Blake: A Traditional View of the Role of the Feminine in Blake's Poetry', *Temenos Academy Review*, 13, 2010, pp 104–121.

3 These lines represent my interpretation of the first several paragraphs of the Kena Upanishad, see for example, *The Upanishads: Breadth of the Eternal*, Trans., Swami Prabhavananda & Frederick Manchester, (Hollywood: Vedanta Press, 1983).

4 See, Laurence Freeman, *Good Heart: A Buddhist Perspective on the Teaching of Jesus*, (Boston: Wisdom Publications, 1998), Introduction.

5 Sogyal Rinpoche, *The Tibetan Book of Living and Dying*, Edited Patrick Gaffney & Andrew Harvey, (London: Rider, 1992).

6 Ibid, pp 46–47.

7 The Zen Master Yoka Daishi (665–713) wrote the Zen Buddhist didactic poem of 64 verses: *Song of Enlightenment*. In the last verse he wrote: 'Don't belittle the sky by looking through a pipe'.

8 All references to Ralph Waldo Emerson in this book are taken from the website: http://www.rwe.org/

9 Elizabeth A. Rauscher & Russell Targ, 'The Speed of Thought: Investigations of a Complex Space-Time Metric to Describe Psychic Phenomena', *Journal of Scientific Exploration*, Vol. 15, No. 3, pp. 331–354, 2001.

10 We can see an example of this confusion in *Scientific American*, 2002: 24.

Chapter 4

1. George A. Miller, *The Science of Mental Life*, (London: Hutchinson, 1962), p 1.
2. I argue this point later in this work and also in *The Meaning of Consciousness*, (Ann Arbor: University of Michigan Press, 1997).
3. The psychological term 'unconscious' is often used in a confusing manner. It is often used to represent what Freud understood to be the subconscious rather than the repressed. In addition, it is usually not distinguished from the 'un-repressed unconscious'. On top of this set of conflicting meanings there is the problem of the 'drive', the basic aspect of the repressed. The 'drive' is a semi-biological referent, which fails to distinguish between what is mental, and what is physical. These conflicting meanings are wrapped up into the psychological terminology of the mind and they represent reasons why I do not apply them. Instead I rely on the terminology of meaning, which is far less confusing.
4. HRH The Prince of Wales, Tony Juniper & Ian Skelly, *Harmony: a new way of looking at our world*, (London: Blue Door, 2010), p 157.

Chapter 5

1. For more details on the circle of learning see, Andrew Lohrey, *Speaking of the Numinous: the meaning of meaning*, (Falmouth: Rishi, 2010), Chapter 9 & 10.

Chapter 6

1. Owen Barfield, *Saving the Appearances: A Study in Idolatry*, (Middletown, Connecticut: Wesleyan University Press, 1988), p 20.
2. *Language Thought and Reality: Selected Writings of Benjamin Lee Whorf*, ed., John B. Carroll, (Massachusetts: MIT Press, 1979), p 214.
3. The view that the body is not its own cause is reflected by such terms as 'biofield', 'epiphenomenon of genome' and 'the Biofield Control System'. These are terms used by some biologists to refer to the organizational field of the body. The Biofield Control System (BCS) is said to control

development, maintenance reproduction and death of the organism. This field includes the mind and it is said to control all aspects of the organism from behaviour to cell activity. The Biological Control system is not, however, based on the order and structure of meaning so there are critical differences between the field contexts of self: *Host, body, culture and symbols* and the field of the BCS. The theory of the BCS tends to relate only to living organisms while the principles at work in the four contexts of being include non-biological, physical systems as well.

4   Elisabeth Kubler-Ross, *On Death and Dying*, (New York: Touchstone Book, 1997).

5   Ibid, p 123.

6   Ibid, pp 40–41.

7   Thich Nhat Hanh, *Zen Keys*, (New York: Anchor Books, 1974), 104.

8   Krishna Das uses this analogy in his DVD: *One Life at a Time*.

9   Rupert Sheldrake: 'Part I – Mind, Memory, and Archetype Morphic Resonance and the Collective Unconscious', *Psychological Perspectives*, 18(1), Spring (1987), pp 9-25.

10 For more on the three stages of maturation see: Andrew Lohrey, *Speaking of the Numinous: the meaning of meaning*, (Falmouth: Rishi, 2010), Part 2.

Chapter 7

1   For a further discussion on this subject see: Andrew Lohrey, *Speaking of the Numinous: the meaning of meaning*, (Falmouth: Rishi, 2010). For Owen Barfield's three-mode model of thought see: Owen Barfield, *Saving the Appearances: A Study in Idolatry*, (Middletown, Connecticut: Wesleyan University Press, 1988).

2   Jacques Lacan, "The subversion of the subject and the dialectic of desire in the Freudian unconscious." In *Écrits: A selection*, trans. Alan Sheridan, (New York: W.W. Norton, 1997).

Chapter 8

1. Joseph Milne, 'Visions of the Cosmos: Nicholas of Cusa and Giordano Bruno', *Temenos Academy Review*, 2011, pp 80–93.
2. W.E.H. Stanner, *The Dreaming & Other Essays*, (Melbourne: Black Inc, 2009), p 57.
3. *Heterogeneity without a norm* is a phrase used by Fredric Jameson, *Postmodernism, or, the Cultural Logic of Late Capitalism*, (Durham: Duke University Press, 1991).
4. Owen Barfield, *Saving the Appearances: A Study in Idolatry*, (Connecticut: Wesleyan University Press, 1988).
5. Owen Barfield, (1988) op cit. p 184.
6. For a detailed explanation of dashboard knowledge see, Owen Barfield, *Poetic Diction: A Study in Meaning*, (Wesleyan Paperback, 1984), pp 23, 24.
7. Albert Camus, *The Myth of Sisyphus*, Trans., Justin O' Brien, (London: Penguin, 2005).

Chapter 9

1. Goleman, D. *Emotional Intelligence*, (New York: Bantam, 1995).
2. Eric Fromm, *The Sane Society*, (London: Routledge, 2002), p 70.
3. Owen Barfield, *Saving the Appearances: A Study in Idolatry*, (Middletown, Connecticut: Wesleyan University Press, 1988), p 110.

Chapter 10

1. How the empty fullness of innocent love relates to the Heart Sutra is a question I do not intend to pursue here. Interpretations of this Sutra are many and sometimes contradictory.
2. Kathleen Raine, *Blake and Tradition*, Vol. 2, (New York: Princeton University Press, 1968), Part VI.

3 Rupert Sheldrake, *The Rebirth of Nature: New Science and the Revival of Animism*, (London: Rider, 1990), p 87.

4 Angela Voss, 'God or the Daemon? Platonic Astrology in the Christian Cosmos, *Temenos Academy Review*, No. 14, 2011, pp 96–116.

5 Robert Stone, *The Secret Life of Your Cells*, (Atglen: Whitford Press, 1989).

6 Christopher Alexander, *The Nature of Order: An Essay on the Art of Building and the Nature of the Universe, Book One*, (Berkeley: The Centre for Environmental Structure, 2002), p 32.

7 'Unconscious Decisions in the Brain', *Nature Neuroscience*, 13 April 2008, www. physorg.com

8 Rupert Sheldrake, *Dogs That Know When Their Owners Are Coming Home, and other unexplained powers of animals*, (London: Arrow, 2000).

9 Henry W. Mayer, *Three Theories of Child Development*, (New York: Harper and Row, 1966).

10 Adam Phillips, *Winnicott*, (London: Fontana, 1988), p 68.

Chapter 11

1 Kathleen Raine, *The Underlying Order and Other Essays*, (London: Temenos Academy, 2008), p 33.

2 Ibid, p 33.

3 Ibid, p 36.

4 Kathleen Raine, *Blake and Tradition*, Volume II, (New York: Princeton University Press, 1968), p 133.

5 Christopher Alexander, *The Timeless Way of Building*, (New York: Oxford University Press, 1979), p. ix.

6 These phrases come from *The Bhagavad Gita*, Chapter 2: (23, 24) Translation and Introduction, Eknath Easwarn, (London: Arkana, 1986).

7 SONNET 116

> Let me not to the marriage of true minds
> Admit impediments. Love is not love
> Which alters when it alteration finds,
> Or bends with the remover to remove:

O no! it is an ever-fixed mark
That looks on tempests and is never shaken;
It is the star to every wandering bark,
Whose worth's unknown, although his height be taken.
Love's not Time's fool, though rosy lips and cheeks
Within his bending sickle's compass come:
Love alters not with his brief hours and weeks,
But bears it out even to the edge of doom.
If this be error and upon me proved,
I never writ, nor no man ever loved

8   *The Upanishads: Breath of the Eternal*, Trans., Swami Prabhavananda & Frederick Manchester, (Hollywood: Vedanta Press, 1983), p 131.
9   Kathleen Raine, (2008) op cit, p 115.

Postscript

1   E.M. Forster, *A Passage to India*, (London: Penguine, 1978), p 283.

Index

Agency, 60
Augustine, Saint, 83
Amma, 17, 21-22, 150
Ardhanari, 49
Asymmetry & non-symmetry, 29

Barfield, Owen, 8, 88, 91, 108, 120-124, 139
Blake, William, 8,
    four-fold vision, 37-53
    doors of perception, 142
Being, 5
Bergson, Henri, 12
Body context, 92
Bohm, David,
    Implicate and explicate orders, 4, 33
Bohm, D. & Hiley. B., 23
Bonaventure Saint, 41

Camus, Albert, 126
Carroll, John, 13
Causality, 32
Circularity, 30
Culture, 87-92

Davies, Paul, 47
Descartes, Rene, 6
Desire, 108-114
Divine humanity, 17
Dualism, 48

Ego, 93, 109
Emerson, Ralph Waldo, 33, 35, 47-49
Emotional intelligence, 135
Empathy, mode of thought, 131-141
Erikson, Erik, 156
Extra-sensory perception, 144

Four-fold meaning, 40
Four modes of thought, 106
Freedom of choice, 66
Freud, Sigmund,
    Conscious, unconscious, 105
Fromm, Eric, 136

Gen Lama, 1-5
Gyuto Monks, 1

Haynes, John-Dylan, 147
Heidegger, Martin, 5

Hobbes, Thomas, 64
Hologram, 16
Human nature, 63

Idols, 91
Illusion, 81-100
Imagination, 8-9
Implicit & explicit mind, 58
Innocent love, 141-159
Intellect, 115-130
Joy, 13
Jung, Carl, 22
Justice, 69

Kubler-Ross, Elizabeth, 94-97, 113, 128

Lacan, Jacques, 111
Language, the prison-house of, 84
Lao Tzu, 16
Laws of meaning, 23-36
Laws of thought, 108
Learning, 71-80
   arc of learning, 73, 116
Lee Whorf, Benjamin, 88
Liberal humanism, 124
Life, 12
Logos, 15
Love, 13

Materialism, 8
Maturation periods, 99

Meaning,
   priority of, 6
   Meaning and meaning, 10
   implicit and explicit, 11
   faces of meaning, 11
Menstrual cycles, 146
Mental life, 55-56
Mechanical science, 45-46, 52
Mind, 11
Millar, George, 55
Mother and child, 156
Moral values, 61

Nature, 43-44
Nicholas of Cusa, 119
Non-local potentials, 26
Nous, 8-9
Now, 27

Omnipotence, 32
Ordinary mind, 57, 81
Origen, 41

Participatory universe, 15
Piaget, Jean, 156
Plenum, 148
Putnam, Robert, 87
Primary perception, 145

Raine, Kathleen, 8, 161-163, 168
Randomness, 22
Readiness-potential, 147-148

Relations – of meaning, 23
Relative autonomy, 62

Sheldrake, Rupert, 34
   on DNA, 99
   morphic resonance, 34
   formative causation, 143
   Dogs That Know When Their Owners Are Coming Home, 155
Skepticism, 118
Single vision, 52
Spirit, 13
Stanner, W.E.H., 119
Symmetry, non-symmetry & asymmetry, 25
Tao, 22
Tibetan Buddhism,
   ordinary mind, 42
Time, 46, 49-51

Unus mundus, 163

Vivekananda, Swami, 17

Winnicott, Donald, 158
Wordsworth, William, 167

Acknowledgments

I would like to express my sincere appreciation:

To Michaela Spencer, for her criticism and suggestions for earlier drafts;

To Cleo, my daughter who has been a critical friend in this endeavour;

To Amanda, whose edits and criticism changed the structure of this book; and

To Michelle Lovi, for her designs and layout and her easy cooperative manner of working.

Notes on the Author

Andrew Lohrey has a PhD in Philosophy from the University of Technology, Sydney. Over the past twenty-five years he has worked as a publisher, writer and applied linguist. Before that he was a member of the Tasmanian Parliament during which time he served as a cabinet minister and Speaker of the House. Andrew Lohrey meditates daily and is a long-term devotee of the south Indian mystic known as Amma. He edited the book by Alex Carey, *Taking the Risk Out of Democracy* and is the author of *The Meaning of Consciousness*, and *Speaking of the Numinous: the meaning of meaning*. Andrew now lives in Tasmania with his wife Amanda. Their website is:

www.spiritualstories.net

www.ingramcontent.com/pod-product-compliance
Lightning Source LLC
Chambersburg PA
CBHW020650300426
44112CB00007B/314